HOW TO WRITE

WELL AT WORK

How to write

WELL AT WORK

Simple steps to get you writing
with fluency and confidence

PETER BARTRAM

A Helping Hand Book

from

New Venture Publishing

First published 2006 as a Helping Hand Book
by New Venture Publishing Ltd
© Peter Bartram 2006

New Venture Publishing Ltd
29 Tivoli Road, Brighton
East Sussex BN1 5BG

E-mail: info@newventurepublishing.co.uk
www.helpinghandbooks.co.uk

ISBN: 0-9552336-2-3
978-0-9552336-2-3

British Library cataloguing-in-publication data
A catalogue record for this book is obtainable from the British Library

Cover design by Mark Tennent
Typeset in Caslon by Mark Tennent, Worthing, West Sussex
Printed and bound by RPM Reprographics Ltd, Chichester, West Sussex

About the author

Peter Bartram is an experienced business writer and journalist who has contributed to a wide range of newspapers and magazines and has written 18 books. His other titles for New Venture Publishing include *How to Write the Perfect Press Release* and *How to Build a Winning Bid Team* (with Carol Kennedy).

CONTENTS

PREFACE

A WAY WITH WORDS

Do you have a way with words?

No doubt you don't have any difficulty putting your point of view when you're talking to colleagues.

But if you're faced with having to make your case in writing, do the words dry up?

If so, you've come to the right place. This is a book for people who want to improve their skills at workplace writing.

Good, fluent writing designed to communicate meaning succinctly and effectively is a powerful business skill in its own right. It's a skill that's in short supply. The official who sent a letter which contained this sentence to a member of the public clearly didn't have a way with words:

I cannot fetter the exercise of my discretion by determining in advance of the exercise of such discretion how I might exercise that discretion.

What he meant was:

I can't tell you what I will decide until I make up my mind.

This solicitor advising a client needed to brush up his writing:

If it is a breach of the rules not to reveal that there have been many breaches of the rules then presumably there must be a further breach of the rules not to reveal the breach of the rules in not revealing the mass breach of the rules, and so on.

What he was trying to say was:

When rules are broken, you have to report the fact. People who fail to report broken rules, break the rule that requires them to do so and should, themselves, be reported as rule-breakers.

And this accountant may have been the greatest bean-counter on earth, but he couldn't clearly explain a client's tax position:

The requirement that deductibility is contingent on expenditure being incurred for the purpose of gaining or producing assessable income is common to the provisions relating to both registration and other expenditure. It does not mean that there must be assessable income arising from the business. All that is required is that the business must be put to use for the ultimate objective of producing assessable income. However, where expenditure is incurred for purposes that include the purpose of producing assessable income, deductibility will only be to the extent that producing assessable income is the purpose for incurring expenditure.

What he was (probably) trying to say was:

With both the registration and other costs of running your company, you can only deduct those expenses that were intended to generate taxable income. You can deduct them providing you genuinely established the business in order to earn taxable income, even if you were not successful in doing so. But if you spent money on something that was only partly related to earning revenue for the business, you can only set off a proportion of its cost against taxable income.

At the very least, poor writing confuses or frustrates those unfortunate enough to receive it. But it may have more serious effects. When Londoners elected a Mayor, 385,952 votes weren't counted because voters hadn't completed their confusing ballot papers correctly. Baffled electors blamed a lack of clear instructions about the single transferable vote system being used in the poll.

Disabled drivers were angry after being fined for not correctly displaying the "blue badges" which allow them to park in restricted areas. Instructions issued by the Department of Transport had told the drivers to display the badge "in such a way that the front of the card is clearly visible" – but without stating which side was the front. The drivers had reasonably, but wrongly, assumed it was the side with their photograph.

When a telephone company sent out a letter setting out details of new tariffs, customers were justifiably confused. The letter contained nearly 40 footnotes about the new tariffs. A team of researchers spent four hours using the letter and information on the telephone company's website trying to work out how much a typical household would pay each quarter for calls – and came up with 36 different answers ranging from £83 to £287.

Poor writing is poor business.

Moreover, good writing is not an optional extra for business. That's because, in many cases, what is written is the business – whether it's a contract, an appointment letter, a memorandum giving instructions to staff, a proposal to a prospective customer or an e-mail apologising for getting it wrong. In all these cases, and hundreds more, writing defines the nature of the transaction. That is why written language lies at the very heart of business – and why it is so important.

So it is not surprising that those employees who succeed in raising their own writing game, also enhance their career prospects. If you can write well at work, you raise your own status in your organisation. You can use your writing skill to influence more people – fellow employees, customers, suppliers, your boss – towards your point of view. If you write well, you become more persuasive and those you deal with will be more likely to take notice.

This, then, is a book for people who understand that the ability to write well at work is good for business – and good for themselves.

Isms, jargon and pc

Yet writing well at work has never been more difficult. In the old days, workplace writing was much easier. You knew what was expected of you. There was a stilted style of business English which combined the passive voice with pompous words derived from Latin, and which spoke in cringingly deferential tones. "Your esteemed communication of the seventeenth ultimo has been received. Your attention is respectfully drawn to…" Uriah Heep, eat your heart out.

Today, workplace writing is more difficult simply because these conventions have disappeared, but there is no universal agreement on what should replace them. Now you have to make your own decisions about what style and tone to adopt. The world of workplace writing is fraught with tricky tactical decisions.

Should you adopt a formal or friendly tone when replying to a long-standing customer who has made a rare complaint? How can you draft a job advertisement so that it attracts the kind of creative management thinker you're looking for without dragging in applications from a host of unsuitable hopefuls? How do you find the serious but tactful tone in the memorandum to your boss suggesting that if he wants to hit the ambitious targets he's set, he should spend more time leading his team and less time on the golf course?

The world of workplace writing throws up an endless variety of different challenges and the old rules provide little guidance. Besides, as a workplace writer, you must be alive to a number of new issues which didn't trouble previous generations.

First, there are the "isms" which you must take care to avoid – sexism, racism and ageism. A regional manager at an employment services firm got the sack after he sent an e-mail to his boss recommending a female colleague for promotion. After detailing her legitimate qualifications for the job, his e-mail added: "And she was a grrrreat shag as well." Ten officers from a police force in the north of England were disciplined for sending racist e-mails. One was headlined "Miss Africa" and showed a gorilla's head superimposed upon the body of a bikini-clad black woman. An employer's advertisement for a new member of staff read: "Young and funky? So are we. Why not join us…" It was for a job that could have been done equally well by a person of any employable age.

Secondly, there is the problem of jargon which, in the last generation, has crept across the face of workplace writing like algae on a lake.

I believe that a cross-pollination of creative properties in multiple media formats with a vertical market approach allows companies to maximise the return for their investment in creative properties and talents and will prove to be the economic engine for our industry in the future

proclaimed one company's chief executive, announcing the signing of an important new contract. This is, unfortunately, typical of much modern business writing which uses pretentious words to make ordinary ideas seem more exciting or important. Thus, "sharing" becomes "cross-pollination", "good ideas" becomes "creative properties" and "source of growth" becomes "economic engine".

There is a place for jargon – and it is in technical literature where the jargon is used because there is no suitable plain English alternative. But the most corrosive effect of jargon is when it replaces simple plain English, not because there isn't a suitable word but because it sounds more fashionable. Thus, "thank you for letting me know" becomes "thank you for the heads-up", and "the price is as much as we can afford" becomes "the price is pushing the envelope". Put them together and a simple sentence

Thank you for letting me know that the price is as much as we can afford

which conveys its meaning clearly becomes:

Thank you for the heads up that the price is pushing the envelope which sounds as though it's written in code and is incomprehensible to anybody who's not familiar with the jargon.

Thirdly, there is the vexed question of handling what's become known as "political correctness". Lapses into political *in*correctness may not appear so much in communications intended for public consumption but have an unfortunate habit of turning up in those which the writer expected to be private. E-mail is the principal carrier of politically incorrect material. A 2005 survey found that 34 per cent of office workers had received sexually explicit or racist e-mails. A second survey revealed that only 52 per cent of companies block racist e-mails.

Critics condemn political correctness as an invention of "thought police". There is even a Campaign Against Political Correctness with a website full of angry little stories about children not being allowed to sing "Baa, Baa, black sheep" at school or office workers refused permission to put up Christmas trees in case they offend people from other religions. But some of their stories have the feel of urban myths.

In fact, the worst excesses of political correctness should more simply be called stupidity. When it comes to writing in the workplace, you need to take a common-sense view of other people's feelings. That doesn't mean you can't use words which the thought police have deemed to be politically incorrect – such as "English" or "black". It does mean that you should be sensitive to the feelings of those who are going to read what you have written. But that's merely extending a core principle of good writing – thinking about your audience and couching what you have to say in language they will find both acceptable and convincing. Think of it as being polite on paper.

Clear words and good business

Despite the problems posed by "isms", jargon and political correctness, when workplace writing fails it is usually because writers haven't taken enough care to convey their meaning clearly enough. Perhaps they were under pressure. Perhaps they didn't fully understand what they were writing. Perhaps they were too lazy to check what they'd written. Whatever the reason, the result is that their organisation loses out. For example, would customers baffled by these instructions on an electrical product be more or less likely to buy another item from the same supplier?

> The switched main live is generally a single black wire and this is connected to the brown wire(s) on the fitting. On a wall light this should be a single red wire. The neutral is generally two black wires and these are connected to the blue wire(s). On a wall light this should be a single black wire. The mains earth wire(s) must be connected to all green/yellow wire(s) or earth terminal on the fitting. When completed ensure that there are no bare or loose strands of wire exposed, and cover all exposed areas of terminal blocks with insulation tape.

In this case, the writer has simply not looked carefully enough at the writing from the reader's point of view. The writer could have made the instructions much more intelligible by separating out information on the "fitting" (whatever it is) and the "wall light", then breaking the installation of each down into numbered steps.

But not all poor workplace writing is the result of lack of thought or care. The unwelcome fact is that much workplace writing is obscure, dense, impenetrable or just plain unreadable because it's meant to be. The writing may be designed to obscure inconvenient facts. Or it may seek to disguise the organisation's true intentions. It may attempt to mislead readers about the organisation's performance. Or it may try to present a false impression of efficiency and success. There are many dishonourable reasons why companies and public bodies seek refuge in weasel words.

If business is a battlefield, then the English language is a weapon in the fight. But it is a weapon that is not always wielded in the cause of clear communication. So when the law forces a supermarket chain to provide information about how it grows its mushrooms, it labels the packaging:

> Mushrooms cultivated on substrate from extensive agriculture which is permitted in organic farming during a transitional period

What it probably means – and the word "probably" is important here – is that the mushrooms are grown in compost from varied sources which doesn't yet fully meet the Soil Association's standards for organic farming. No doubt there are many customers who buy the mushrooms who don't read the packaging. But as customers become more concerned about whether products have been produced organically and ethically, they will increasingly opt for products which provide the information they need in clear English.

Creating a verbal obstacle course for customers at any time they deal with you is not good for business. That is particularly true in any communication which has financial implications. So this note from an airline about the circumstances in which passengers can claim refunds, is not likely to have pleased passengers seeking their money back:

Note – cancellations – before departure fare is refundable. If combining a non-refundable fare with a refundable fare only the Y/C/J-class half return amount can be refunded. After departure fare is refundable. If combining a non-refundable fare with a refundable fare refund the difference/if any/between the fare paid and applicable normal… oneway fare.

When people deal with any organisation, they generally want a straight answer to a simple question. So when one customer asked a company whether it still sold blank CDs, the e-mailed reply:

We are currently in the process of consolidating our product range to ensure that the products that we stock are indicative of our brand aspirations. As part of our range consolidation we have also decided to revisit our supplier list and employ a more intelligent system for stock acquisition. As a result of the above certain product lines are now unavailable through [this company], whilst potentially remaining available from more mainstream suppliers

could, more helpfully, have been a simple "no".

Happily, more organisations, especially those alive to their social responsibility obligations, do appreciate the need to communicate clearly. They realise that good writing is essential if they want to win a reputation for openness. Clear writing, not weasel words, will be a hallmark of those companies that win a reputation for ethical business.

A WRITING SKILLS SHORTAGE

At the very time more organisations realise they need to improve the quality of their writing, they find that not enough employees have the skills to do so.

If various studies are to be believed, literacy standards among the working population are depressingly low – and falling. Nearly half the UK workforce – 12 million people – struggle with reading and writing skills no better than those expected of a child leaving primary school, according to a 2006 report by the House of Commons' Public Accounts Committee. Edward Leigh MP, the PAC's chairman, summed up the problems this causes: "The low level of literacy and numeracy in the adult population is bad for national productivity and bad for those individuals who may struggle to cope with work and daily living."

Sadly, there doesn't seem much prospect of any swift improvement. Another report, published by Cambridge Assessment, part of the University of Cambridge Local Examinations Syndicate (also in 2006), contained depressing findings. It revealed that the number of spelling mistakes in the GCSE papers of pupils gaining A to E grades had more than doubled between 1980 and 2004. In all, one in 50 of the words in the average examination script was spelt wrongly. Errors included "unaturaly" for "unnaturally", "inevitabely" for "inevitably" and "shear" for "sheer".

Worse still, street slang had began to creep into written work, where it had no place. So teachers marking exam papers encountered terms such as "dead good" instead of "very good" and "real keen" instead of "really keen". "Whilst non-standard English is used much more frequently by candidates awarded lower grades, it is now also sometimes found in writing by candidates awarded highest grades," noted the Cambridge report.

Does all this evidence mean that attempts to raise the standard of workplace writing are doomed to fail?

It does not.

Where employers and employees work together to improve the quality of corporate writing, they can achieve excellent results. The annual awards of the Plain English Campaign provide a showcase for some of the finest workplace writing in Britain. Many other organisations strive to gain the coveted Crystal Mark, awarded by the Plain English Campaign, on their written output. To date, the Mark has appeared on more than 10,000 documents.

But there is no escaping the fact that enhancing the quality of written work depends on individuals improving their own workplace writing skills.

Writing in the digital age

If you want to improve the standard of your own workplace writing, you will be doing so at a time when the very nature of written English is, itself, changing. Just as old standards have disappeared, so new technologies have emerged to shape the future of workplace writing.

There used to be a decent distance between spoken and written English. But mobile phone texting and e-mails have shrunken that distance in the minds of a generation of workplace writers. We now need to ask the question: when is the written word not the written word?

Take the text message. Is it supposed to be condensed written English – a digital age version of telegramese – or a kind of coded cybertalk? "GR8 2CU," uses written characters to convey phonetic sounds. Yet it's undeniably useful when you have only a small keypad to work on – the message takes only seven keystrokes, including the space, instead of 16 for "Great to see you".

Then there is e-mail, probably the most pervasive influence on workplace writing. Do you look on e-mails as taking the place of a letter or a telephone call? The salutation you use could provide the answer. If you start "Dear..." you probably think letter. If you begin "Hi..." you may think phone call. Whichever is the case, e-mails have developed as a communication medium in which it's acceptable to use the vernacular and adopt a free-and-easy way with grammar and punctuation. But as e-mails are the medium in which workplace writers write most often, we shouldn't be surprised when the informal or just plain sloppy English of e-mails makes an appearance in documents where a more formal and structured approach to language is expected.

The computer revolution has had a profound impact on the way people write. When people used pen and ink or typewriters, it was difficult and time-consuming to make changes. You had to rewrite a whole page or type a new document. So you thought carefully about what you were going to write before putting it down on paper.

Writing on screen is a different kind of creative process. Instead of working out in your mind what you want to say before committing it to paper, you try it out on screen, knowing it's easy to change if you don't like it. As a result, you can work faster, using the screen as though it were an extra lobe of your brain. You can put your first thoughts down, rather than your second, knowing that it's almost as easy to change them on screen as in your mind.

That's fine, if you improve your draft in the light of your second, or third, thoughts. But if you work in a busy office with the in-tray full and the next job pressing – and which of us doesn't? – there's a danger you let the first thoughts stand. So writing on screen can produce a "good enough" approach. And the problem is that, too often, what's deemed "good enough", isn't.

But this is a book which focuses on solutions rather than problems. It's not a book that believes the English language is a sacred monument with which the untutored should not tamper. It starts from the premise that the English language belongs to the people and that they are the sole custodians of how it can be used. English is a living language. It evolves from generation to generation – these days, from year to year. If it didn't we'd still be walking around saying: "Take thou this groat for bearing yon fardels thither, my good coz."

The remainder of this book focuses on practical advice which should help you to become a better workplace writer. In part one, Perfect Business Writing, we explore, first, how you can conquer the demon of "writing paralysis". Then we look at the six steps that should have you writing with fluency and confidence. We also show how you can adapt your writing to the people you're aiming it at and how you can adopt the most appropriate style. Finally, we'll discover how to lay out written work more effectively and avoid the most common grammatical traps.

In part two, The Perfect Report, we'll build on the basics to find out how to write a report – whether just a few pages or a lengthy document. We'll discover how to get started, how to find the information you might need and how to draw effective conclusions to include in your report. Then we'll explore how to write up your report so that you will impress the people who read it.

Writing in the workplace doesn't have to be a cross between fear and tedium. If you know how to tackle the writing assignments you're given, you'll enjoy completing them. And the pleasure you get from your work will shine through in its quality. You will discover that you do, after all, have a way with words. That will be good for your organisation – and it won't do any harm to your career prospects.

Part i

Perfect business writing

CHAPTER 1

A CURE FOR WRITING PARALYSIS

PUT IT IN WRITING

Do those words strike terror into your heart? The scene is all too familiar. You've had a good idea that could bring more business to your company, cut costs or improve administrative efficiency. You mention it to your boss. He seems to like the idea. Then he utters those dreaded words. Suddenly, the idea that should have helped you make a mark doesn't seem so hot. After all, writing is hard work. Perhaps you try to put your thoughts on paper. But your idea somehow seems less compelling on paper than it did when you first mentioned it. Best forget it after all?

Forget writing and you can forget chances of career advancement. Few people rise high in major organisations without the ability to express themselves well in writing. Civil servants have a phrase for it. He (or she) is "good" on paper. It means they are able to describe a state of affairs or set out a course of action convincingly in writing. In organisations where decisions and actions must be justified in writing, such a person will excel. And such organisations exist as much in the private as in the public sector.

Why is writing important?

Perhaps writing seems not too important in your job. You spend most of your time meeting customers, managing other staff or in meetings. Yet in almost all jobs, writing will play some role and the ability to write clearly and effectively will help you to perform that job better. Good writing is important both for you and your company.

For you, good writing:

- Helps you to communicate more effectively with other people in your working life.
- Improves your status in the eyes of people who only know you through what you write.
- Advances your career prospects because you are seen by superiors to be effective in advancing your ideas.

For your company, good writing:

- Contributes to business success by improving communication between employees and with customers, suppliers and business partners.
- Creates, along with other factors, a corporate image of the organisation.
- Advances the process of planning and decision making by ensuring that all interested people are lucidly informed of relevant facts and opinions.

In the final analysis, the ability to write well will often be a touchstone, a means of judging whether you are worthy of further advancement. Indeed, good writing can even determine whether you get the job in the first place, for plenty of otherwise well qualified job-seekers have been rejected because they submitted poor application letters.

Writing paralysis: the disease

What is it about a blank sheet of paper? It can have the same sort of mesmerising effect as a snake on a rabbit. You know just what you want to say, but as soon as you reach for your scratch pad and pen your mind goes blank. Somehow, the ideas which were so clear in your mind won't flow smoothly down your arm, through your hand and on to the paper. You have the classic symptom of writing paralysis.

It helps to understand what causes writing paralysis because then it is easier to cure the condition. One reason is not being able to think of anything to say. And if that is the problem, the cure lies in spending more time researching and thinking about what you have to write about.

In most cases, however, you have plenty to say. Instead the main cause of your writing paralysis is trying to think of too many things at the same time. This can best be explained by considering a meeting to discuss the drafting of a report. If the meeting is badly chaired, everybody will start chipping in with their ideas in a haphazard way. Consider some of the points that might be raised:

- Are we going to split the report into sections?
- Should we write it in the first or third person?
- Will we print it on both sides of the paper?
- Should we have a summary at the start?
- Will we include diagrams, charts or tables?
- What recommendations do we want to make?
- Who should we circulate the report to?
- How much technical detail do we need to include?
- Do we want to number the paragraphs?

All these questions – and many others – need consideration but not in the order mentioned. Writing paralysis is too often caused by trying to think about all these issues at the same time, instead of in a structured and logical way. When you suffer from writing paralysis, your brain is like this meeting in which too many unrelated questions are being raised in the wrong order. What you lack is framework in which to consider your writing task.

Writing paralysis: the cure

The starting point for any business writing task is to consider some fundamental questions. Answer these questions and you have created a framework in which to approach the writing task.

Why do I need to write something? Business writing is not recreational. Nor is it intended for entertainment or diversion. All business writing should achieve a purpose. The writing is an act of creation – of a letter, memo, report, statement and so on – which should achieve a result. If you know what result you want to achieve, you will identify the reason for writing. Often the need to write is triggered by somebody else's action:

- A customer complains.
- A prospect asks for a quotation.
- An applicant applies for a job.
- A manager calls for a report.
- A colleague requests information.

When this happens, the purpose of your writing task is often clear. In other cases, the task may be more complex and the results you need to achieve less obvious. However, if you start by defining what result you want to achieve, the purpose of your writing task will become much clearer in your mind.

What is the most appropriate form for my writing? Having defined the purpose of your writing task, you now need to decide the most appropriate format for the document you produce. You could produce your document in a large number of formats. Some of the most common are:

- Letter
- Memorandum
- Report
- Minute
- Note
- Statement

In most cases, the form of the document you produce will be fairly clear from the task. If a manager asks for a report, he expects to see the document in report format, not as a long letter. But perhaps the manager just calls for information about a specific topic. Should you send it in a letter, memo or report? You need to consider the scope of the task. You must decide how much information you need to provide in order to achieve the result you want.

Take the case of the customer complaint. Perhaps the customer has a simple moan, such as late delivery. You can handle this task with a letter setting out the reasons for the late delivery, what you are doing to prevent it happening again and, finally, apologising for the inconvenience caused. At a more complex level, a major customer might be complaining about the level of service he has received from your company over a period of time. He catalogues his complaints in detail. In this instance, you might want to send him a report on all the issues he raises, adding your perspective, and describing the measures you are taking to improve service to him. You would send the report with a shorter covering letter.

The lesson: if you decide at the outset the form that your document should take, you will have cleared one of the big decisions about it out of the way. Moreover, because you would write a letter in a completely different way from, say, a report, you have solved your concern about how to draft the document.

Who am I writing to? This question is important because its answer influences the approach and tone of your document. For example, a letter to your boss will be succinct. Your ideas and opinions will be packaged with soothing phrases – "It is possible that... I would like to suggest..." – designed to make them seem less abrasive. You will not bother with such phrases in a letter to a subordinate. Nor might you be so concerned to write a short letter. You subordinate's time is of less value than your boss's.

The same approach applies to all your writing. A letter to a complaining customer needs a different tone than a letter to a satisfied customer. A report to a body of technical experts will require a completely different approach to a report on the same subject to a lay audience. The lesson: defining your audience, whether one person or a larger number, will help you decide how to approach your writing task.

What information do I need to provide? It may seem strange that this is the last rather than the first question. But if you have answered the previous three questions you will have already created a framework in which it is easier to decide on the information to include and leave out:

- You know why you have to write the document – so the purpose is clear in your mind.
- You know the form your document will take – letter, memo,

report, etc – which helps you understand the level and detail of information you need to provide.

- You know who is to read the document – so you can judge the level at which to pitch your writing and the tone to adopt.

With these points in mind, you can focus on the specific information you need to include in your document. You will find it helpful to answer these questions:

- What information will the reader expect from this document?
- Do I already have that information?
- If not, where can I get the information?
- How much detail should I include?
- Will I need to explain technical terms or does the reader already understand them?
- Out of all the information I provide, what are the key points to stress?

One final point: do not fear writing paralysis or feel you are the only sufferer. All writers suffer from it from time to time. What is important is knowing how to cure it when it strikes. Having a clear framework – summarised in the four main questions above – provides a way of breaking through the block. Soon your words will be flowing on to paper.

Document benchmarks

As we have seen, getting started is half the battle, but knowing the standards you ought to aim for is also important. Over the past few years, business has spent millions of pounds in "total quality" campaigns. But, too often, one of the most important elements of business is ignored in the quality drive – the standard of the written word. Just how do you assess the "quality" of a letter? How do you determine the excellence of a report? Does it all come down to a subjective opinion or are there any benchmarks to guide you? When you write in business, just what standards should you aim for?

Here are six:

Clear purpose. Whatever the document, it should be clear from the top of the first page what its purpose is. When the recipient asks the question "why have I received this document?" the answer should be immediately obvious.

Complete. The document should contain all the information the reader could reasonably want. No glaring omissions, but…

Concise. The reader should not feel deluged with detail. You should pitch the document at the right level, bearing in mind the background knowledge of your reader and his position within his organisation.

Accurate. Which means checking facts and proof reading carefully.

Logically presented. The information should be in the most appropriate order. The document should read clearly. If you are making a case, you should develop your argument from point to point and support it with relevant facts.

Looks good on the page. There are documents that are inviting to read and documents that repel the reader. Nobody reads business documents for fun, so why make it difficult? Make it easy and become a more successful business writer. Set out the document attractively and woo the recipient to read it.

On all these points, more in subsequent chapters. For now, test the last document you wrote against these six factors. Did it measure up?

A personal writing manifesto

Is it possible to become a better writer? In most cases, the answer is "yes", but not without some effort. Most business people will then ask themselves the question, is the effort worth it? Few people deny that training in specialist skills is worthwhile. People spend years training to become an accountant, a lawyer, a personnel officer or a production manager. But they too often resent the effort needed to become a better writer. Yet improved writing skills would make them a more effective accountant, lawyer, personnel officer or production manager.

For the individual who wants to become a better business writer, here is a personal manifesto:

- I will invest some time to improve my writing. Start by studying this book and spending some time putting the lessons into practice.
- I will be more constructively critical. Both of the writing I do and the material I read.
- I will ask a close and trusted colleague to help me identify the main weaknesses in my writing. Then I will try to rectify them, if necessary by seeking professional help.
- I will not send out a document I am not completely happy with. I will spend more time to bring it up to the benchmark standards.
- I will make it clear to my staff that effective written communications stimulates efficiency and improves the image of our business. I will help them to develop their own writing improvement programmes.

And finally:

- I will keep the promises I have made in my business writing manifesto.

Chapter 2

Six steps to successful writing

Writing for action

As we have seen, business writing is writing with a purpose. When you write, the aim is to achieve a result. The number of different writing assignments you might have to undertake is potentially huge. For example:

- Report on a budget overspend
- Letter answering customer complaint
- Circular to staff about Christmas holiday arrangements
- Letter of appointment
- Letter of dismissal
- Leaflet about new product
- Statement for the chairman to read at the agm
- Press release about opening of new branch
- Factory board notice about shopfloor untidiness
- Article about your department for staff newspaper
- Marketing plan for a new product
- Instruction manual on operating new product
- Speech to local chamber of commerce
- Letter handing in your resignation

All these seem completely different. So can there possibly be a common approach? In fact, the same basic approach will serve you well, no matter what the nature of your writing assignment.

The six step approach

First, think. Even before you put pen to paper you need to understand what the assignment involves. You need to ask the four questions designed to clear away writing paralysis. The thinking phase can take a few seconds in the case of a reply to simple letter. Alternatively, it might take a few days if you have been asked to produce a report on a multi-million pound building project, a detailed marketing proposal or a business plan for launching a new subsidiary. If the assignment is of significant size, you need to divide the thinking phase into a number of a sections.

The scope of the project. You need to make sure you understand the scope of the assignment and what is expected at the end of it. In doing this, you may need to ask the person who gave you the assignment some questions. Those questions could include:

- What kind of document do they expect?
- Who will be reading the document?
- What sort of decisions might they want to take on the basis of its contents?
- How much detail would they like to receive?
- When do they want the document delivered?

How you will tackle the project. You need to gain an idea of how you will set about producing and delivering the document within the time available. In order to do this, you need answers to more questions:

- Is the timescale for document delivery realistic?
- How much time will writing the document take?
- Will I need to involve other people in gathering information

or writing sections of the document?

- Will other people need to be involved in approving the document before it is delivered?
- How will the document be produced? (For example, will you write by hand and ask a secretary to type it or will you key it straight on to a word processor?)

From this thinking phase, you should develop an outline plan for tackling the assignment. In the case of a simple task, such as replying to a letter, the answers to these questions should fall into place easily. In the case of a longer and more complex task, you may want to write down an outline plan of how you will tackle the task. With your plan clear, you move on to stage two.

Second, gather information. Except in the simplest of cases, it is unlikely that you will have all the information you need to complete an assignment at your fingertips. Even writing a letter in response to a customer query could involve gathering information from a number of sources – for example, a sales person, the accounts department and a distribution depot. Writing a large document could involve an extensive information gathering exercise.

Information gathering is such an important process in writing that it can make or mar a document. Yet, too often, information gathering gets skimped. The result is the reply to a customer query that doesn't deal with all the points raised (which generates further correspondence). Or inadequate cost data in a report (which causes a meeting to be adjourned pending further enquiries). Or a failure to provide sufficient detail in a sales proposal (which means the business is lost).

The information you gather for a document can be of two types – facts and opinions. The facts are usually the backbone of the document, but the opinions can also be important for they colour the way a reader receives the facts and the conclusions he may draw from them. Facts and opinions are often linked together in the writing of the document. Facts support opinions. (Sometimes, opinions go in search of facts.) Gathering both is not always as easy as it sounds.

Facts. On the face of it, a fact is a fact. Yet life is often not that simple. A fact is only a fact if it is correct. Too often, "facts" come second, third or even fourth hand. This means that when you are gathering facts for your document, you need to be alive to the reliability of the source that supplies the information. Both people and published sources can let you down. Managers, for example, who seem to be in command of their department, sometimes turn out only to have a hazy idea of some facts.

How can you tell whether information you collect is accurate or not? There are a few danger signs to watch for, and you find those signs in the way people give you the information. In particular, beware of vagueness:

- I think it is around 20%.
- We have about half a dozen competitors in that market.
- That branch was opened two or three years ago.

In practice, "around 20%" could means anything from 10% to 30%, "half a dozen" could be as many as 10, "two or three years ago" might be four years ago. Of course, it might be the case that you only need a rough idea. Generalities might be enough, but if you need facts for your documents, they must be precise and accurate and you must make the effort to make them so.

Just because it is in print, doesn't make it a "fact" either. Of course, some sources are more reliable than others. You would regard a half-year projection of full-year income from your own accounts department as accurate but you might know a newspaper's speculation about that figure to be wide of the mark. Why, then, should you believe the same newspaper's prediction of another company's likely out-turn?

The point about this is that facts need to be gathered thoroughly. There is no need to become paranoid about fact gathering, or to disbelieve everything you read or are told. Instead, you need to apply the qualities of persistence, healthy scepticism and common sense to fact gathering. And if you are not sure about a fact – check. There is little that will undermine your writing more than demonstrably wrong facts.

Opinions. Much business writing involves expressing opinions. Sometimes you will be expressing your own opinions, sometimes other people's. So, often, finding out and understanding other people's opinions will be an important part of the information gathering process. You could find yourself gathering other people's opinions in two main ways.

Others' opinions: In this case, your writing assignment involves you expressing somebody else's opinion. You may already know what that opinion is, or you may have to find out about it in hard and detailed terms. Instances of this include:

- Drafting a note about a discussion by other people.
- Preparing a speech for the chairman.
- Writing a letter for signature by your boss.

Your opinions: In this case, the final views expressed in the document will be yours, but you want them to be influenced by the opinions of others, perhaps colleagues in your organisation or outside experts. You need to understand not only what opinion somebody holds, but why he holds it. Why he holds the opinion will help you to fit it into the context of your own thinking and give weight to it. Examples of working in this way include:

- Finding out market researchers' views on the growth of sales as background for a marketing plan.
- Discovering the opinions of shop-floor staff on the reliability and effectiveness of machinery for a report on improving manufacturing efficiency.
- Asking a supervisor's opinion of the people in his department for a staff assessment.

When gathering information, you need to pay particular attention to collecting information that will support the points you make in what you write. When you have the information to hand, you need to organise it before you start writing, which brings us to step number three.

Third, plan. Even in the simplest writing task – sending a memo, for example – a moment's planning pays dividends. In a larger writing assignment – producing a report, perhaps – planning is essential before you start to write. In the planning phase, you must decide how the information you need to convey in order to achieve the result you want can best be presented. In other words, you need to work out the overall structure of your document.

In a short document, such as a letter, this may just mean noting the topics you plan to deal with in each paragraph and the order you propose to deal with them. For a longer document, you may have to draw up a detailed outline. Drawing up an outline for a report can seem daunting when you have a lot of information to include. So it is useful to have a formula for planning a report. In nine cases out of ten you will be able to draw up a workable outline using not more than three levels of detail:

Top level: These are the main subject areas you will be dealing with in the report, rather akin to the chapters in a book. For example, a report on sales opportunities in Europe, might take the different countries as the main subject areas. A report on moving to a new office might have subject areas dealing with accommodation at the new factory, timetable for the move, resources needed for moving, impact on existing workloads, and so on.

The art of defining these subject areas is to see the big issues you need to deal with in the report. You need to write the subject areas as a list. Leave plenty of space between each item on the paper, so you could add more information to each as you work up your outline in more detail. When you have done so, ask yourself whether everything you need to say can be accommodated within one of the subject areas. If it can, then you have defined all the main subject areas you need for the report. If not, think through the overall structure again, and decide whether you need other main subject headings.

Middle level: Within each subject area, you will need to deal with a number of topics. So once you have defined your subject areas, you need to take each in turn and break it down into topics. A topic is a self-contained piece of information that is essential if the reader is to gain a full understanding of the subject. For example, in the sales opportunities in Europe report, you might have a subject area for Germany and topic areas for west Germany, east Germany and Bavaria. Alternatively, you might divide your report into topic areas for each of your product lines available in the German market.

Similarly, the "resources needed for moving" subject area of the report on the office move could include topic areas on legal services, removal firms, utilities and services, new stationery, and so on. In each subject area you should make a list of the topics you need to deal with. Again, ask yourself whether you have included everything that a reader will want to know.

Depending on the size of your report, you may feel that planning the subject and topic areas is sufficient. However, in large reports you may want your plan to cover a third level of detail:

Lower level: Within each topic area, you might want to list the specific information you must include. For example, in the sales report example, under west Germany you might want to refer to your branches in Hamburg, Cologne and Dusseldorf. The utilities section of the office moving report could have paragraphs dealing with electricity, gas and telephones.

Although this may seem fairly obvious, many writers plunge into reports without giving enough thought to the planning. Planning is important because it forces you to think through in detail everything you want to deal with in the report. Moreover, it also makes you think about the best order for dealing with the main subjects, and within subjects with the different topics. This means that you can move the subjects and topics around into a new structure before you start to write the report. If you create such as a plan, you should find writing the report easier, partly because you will have thought out the structure in advance and partly because you will have broken down what is a large job into bite-sized chunks.

Fourth, write. Now comes the task of getting your information down on paper. There are a number of techniques that can help you make the writing easier. As these are dealt with in detail in subsequent chapters, we move on to the next stage.

Fifth, review. This is a stage which is most often ignored by business writers. At a simple level, it means reading through what you have just written to make sure it says what you want it to say. When reviewing your own writing, you need to check at different levels and answer a number of questions:

Have I dealt with my brief fully? If you had a written brief, now is the time to re-read it quickly to make sure you have covered all the points. If you are replying to a letter you should glance through it again, to make sure you have answered all the points. A high proportion of written documents fall short of what is needed because they fail to deal with all the issues required of them.

Have I written to achieve the results I want? At the outset, you should have had a clear idea what you wanted your document to achieve. For example, if you are replying to a customer complaint you want to answer the specific queries raised, create a situation where the customer continues to do business with you… and apologise. In a report, you want to ensure that your recommendations and the information supporting them are clear.

Have I written clearly? You should have written so that your document can be easily read and understood. You should avoid using incoherent or ugly sentences (of which more later).

Are there any grammatical, spelling or punctuation errors which need correcting? (Again, more of these later.)

Is the document properly addressed, titled, dated and signed? Almost all documents have to say where they have come from and to whom they are aimed. Yet sometimes such information is left out.

In some cases, you may find that your document needs to be

reviewed by other people before it can be issued. For example, you might have drafted a letter for your boss. In a more complex case, the members of a working party might want to review the draft of a document before it is submitted to the board or a management committee. In instances such as these, it is advisable to produce your document with double-spacing so that the revisers can more easily write in suggested alterations.

Sixth, revise. Where you are solely responsible for your document, you should make any changes to it as you ask yourself the five questions above. Doing this requires a certain self critical ability. If you start from the position that your work is so wonderful it can never be improved, you will never revise successfully. Samuel Johnson recalled the advice of a college tutor: "Read over your compositions, and wherever you meet with a passage which you think is particularly fine, strike it out." That is saying you need to beware of being seduced by your own eloquence.

Sometimes you will have to incorporate other people's suggestions and amendments into your document. You may find that your revisers amend a document exactly, deleting and adding words with precision. In other cases, they write cryptic comments in the margin, often in equally cryptic handwriting. This happens when they want something changed but are too lazy to think of the appropriate form of words to express it as they want it. However, while your colleagues can expect you to be a good writer, they cannot expect you to be a mind reader. So if your document needs to be reviewed by others, it is a good idea to ask them to make any precise changes they want to the manuscript, rather than general comments.

Can these six steps really help you write better business documents? The answer is yes. The six steps provide you with a framework for approaching a writing assignment in a logical and structured way. After completing the six steps you can be more confident you have considered all aspects of your task and produced a document which is fit for purpose.

CHAPTER 3

HITTING THE TARGET

KNOW YOUR READER

No business writing is done in a vacuum. It is part of a process of communication which involves transferring information from one person to another. Before you start to write, you need to focus your thoughts on your reader for two main reasons. First, you want to tune what you write as far as possible on to his wavelength of understanding.

Secondly, you want to make what you write as persuasive as possible to your reader. Your document may be aimed at one person, a small group or a large audience of many different types of people. Even when what you write will be read by many people, you still need to give some thought as to the audience you are writing for. You need to hit the target. And that involves understanding what kind of writing will be most acceptable to your reader.

You can understand your reader more by considering two sets of opposites – in and out, up and down.

In and out

The first point to consider is whether you are writing to somebody inside or outside your organisation. This is important because it will affect:

The way you address them. In general, you can write more succinctly to somebody inside your organisation than outside (but see up and down below). Some of the verbal massage and communication niceties that you would use for an external communication are not always needed internally. Consider a simple example – replying to a query about whether a particular product is in stock. Internally, you might reply:

Memorandum
Dear George,
Thanks for your memo of (date). We have 50 dishwashers left at Ruislip and 20 at Wallsend.
Regards,
Peter.

This is short, brief, friendly, but provides the essential information requested. However, a reply to a customer could run like this:

Letter
Dear Mr Smith (or Fred if you know him well).
Thank you for your letter of (date) about the immediate availability of dishwashers. We currently have 50 machines in stock at our Ruislip warehouse and 20 at Wallsend.
Please let me know if you require any further information.
Yours sincerely,
Peter Jones
Sales Manager.

This is a simple example, but it points out some important differences:

- George only needs a memo, Mr Smith requires a proper topped and tailed letter.

- George's memo keeps the greetings and sign off to a friendly minimum. It also assumes George is fully aware of the subject of his original enquiry. The letter to Mr Smith reminds him of the query.
- The memo and letter assume different levels of knowledge. George knows that Ruislip and Wallsend are warehouses. Mr Smith doesn't.
- Mr Smith's letter invites a further enquiry if needed, to stress the company is keen to provide service.

The tone you use. The tone of the language you use can be quite different depending on whether you are writing to somebody inside your organisation rather than outside. Consider these next two examples, circular letters about the closure of the company car park.

To all staff:
The car park will be closed all day on Monday 5 January for essential repairs and maintenance. Alternative parking is available at the town centre car parks, but staff should note that these tend to become full after 9.30am. The company car park will reopen at 7.00am on Tuesday 6 January. June Smith (extension 0000) is coordinating the operation and can provide more information.

To all customers:
Would you please note that our car park will be closed all day on Monday 5 January? This is so that essential repairs and maintenance can be carried out. Although there is alternative parking available in the town centre car parks, these become full after

9.30am. If you are planning to visit the offices, it may be more convenient if you could arrange your visit on another day. The car park will open again at 7.00am on Tuesday 6 January. We apologise if these arrangements cause you any inconvenience. If you require any further information please call June Smith on (telephone number).

The differences here are clear but crucial:

- The staff memo adopts a succinct tone. All the information is included, but it is not dressed up with soothing phrases ("it may be more convenient"). The memo is saying: look these are the facts and they affect us all.
- The customer memo is phrased in a softer tone. The information is presented in a way that seems to minimise the impact of the car park closure. Unlike the staff memo, it offers a specific apology for the inconvenience. The customer memo is saying: we have to do this, but we will reduce the inconvenience to you as much as possible.
- The level of understanding you assume your reader has about the subject matter of your communication. This is important because it will influence the amount of information you put into your document. A useful way of thinking about this aspect is whether your reader has more, less or about the same knowledge of the subject matter as you.

More: In this case you can use specialised terms and concepts confidently knowing that your reader will understand them. You should try to write in a tone that gently acknowledges your lesser knowledge of the subject. This means make the document less assertive than if you are writing to someone with the same or a lesser level of knowledge than you. For example:

A In my opinion, the economy will grow by four per cent in the next financial year.

B According to a study by the Institute for Economic Affairs, the economy will grow by four per cent in the next financial year.

In A, you are making a dogmatic assertion about the growth of the economy, which might seem arrogant to your reader if you are not a trained economist. Your reader might disagree and wonder about your qualifications for making such a confident statement. In B you shift responsibility for the opinion from yourself to somebody else – in this case an undeniably expert body. B sounds less assertive. Equally important, if B reflects your private opinion, it is a more effective way of putting it across to somebody at a higher level in the corporate hierarchy.

The same: In this case, you can pitch your communication at a level that you would feel comfortable with if you were the reader instead of the writer. However, it is important to bear in mind that not all people are exactly the same. You may have some areas of special knowledge that your reader lacks, so you should bear in mind the lessons below:

Less: In this case, the judgement is how much lower? How much background knowledge will your reader already have of the subject you are writing about? If you are to write effectively, you must provide enough background information for your reader to understand and make a judgement on the subject matter of your document. For example:

A The growth of Unix means we should consider porting our own applications to open platforms.

B The growth in use of the Unix standard in software means we should consider moving our own software applications on to computers which handle the open systems standards which Unix represent.

To a non-computer literate reader, A is a string of impenetrable jargon. With B, more information is introduced to help the reader understand what is written. Unix is described as a "standard in software" and "open platforms" becomes "computers which handle the open systems standards", more comprehensible even if the reader doesn't know what open systems standards are. Finally, a jargon term "porting" becomes "moving", which has a plain English meaning.

The vocabulary you use. In the end, your document comes down to words. Will your reader understand the words you use? This question is related to the level of understanding and, again, requires careful thought and fine judgement. For example, all the borrowers of a building society could be expected to understand the meaning of the word "mortgage" but perhaps not the term "endowment mortgage". Except that most holders of endowment mortgages would understand the term.

The test to apply is whether your reader is likely to have had personal experience of the vocabulary your are using. You need to ask the question: is it reasonable to assume that my reader will know what this word means?

Up and down

Now let's consider up and down communications, which applies mostly to written material within an organisation. This boils down to a simple proposition: an employee will write to his boss in a different tone to the way his boss writes to him. Yet although the tone of up and down writing is different, much friction is caused in the business world by the failure of managers and staff to appreciate the qualities of effective up and down communications. Let us start with communications that go up the organisation. Take this example:

Memorandum from section leader to boss.
For the third time this week, the computer network has crashed. It was off the air for three hours and, as a result, 170 orders could not be despatched the same day. If the network continues to crash, I can give no guarantee that we will be able to maintain our same-day despatch policy.

This memo seems to the point. It states the problem and the consequence. It is certainly not wordy or unclear. The problem is that it is just a bit too much to the point. The network crashing is a problem for the boss as well as the section leader and this memo is likely to ruffle his feathers. Moreover, although it may not be the section leader's job to find a solution to the crashing network, the memo is purely negative. The section leader hasn't appreciated some of the diplomatic points of upward communications.

The following approach might have smoothed the boss's feathers and earned some kudos for the section leader:

Memorandum from section leader to boss.
The network crash yesterday put our section's computers out of action for three hours. Although we worked until just before

the last post was despatched, we still had 170 orders unfulfilled. As you will know, these network problems are making it difficult for us to maintain our same-day despatch policy. Although we cannot change the network, there are some alterations to working practices that would make this section less vulnerable to computer down-time...

This memo is altogether softer in tone and, equally important, adopts a constructive standpoint. The first memo's subtext is saying to the boss: "Here is my problem. You do something about it." The second memo's subtext is saying: "Here is a problem we share. May I suggest some ways of tackling it." Not only is the second more effective as a piece of communication, it is more likely to result in a solution of the underlying problem.

What lessons do these memos tell us about up-organisation communication? There are four main points:

First, the tone needs to reflect the relative position of the writer and the reader of the communication. It needs to be tactful rather than assertive. It needs to employ massaging phrases such as "you may not be aware" or "I'm sure you'll agree". But there is no need to hark back to Victorian times ("I remain, Sir, your most humble and obedient servant").

Secondly, the communication should be positive rather than negative. The higher up the organisation the more problems the reader will have. The writer scores brownie points by suggesting (not demanding) solutions. (Former prime minister Margaret Thatcher was said to choose her cabinet ministers partly on the basis of people who brought her solutions rather than problems.)

Thirdly, personal opinions should be presented in a low-key manner. The wise chief executive knows that most staff, no matter how lowly, have useful ideas to contribute. But he will bristle if a junior clerk tries to tell him how to run his company.

Fourthly, the specific facts senior managers need should be provided. Too often junior members of staff forget that their bosses – and their bosses' bosses – are not immersed in the sharp-end detail. The boss may miss the significance of what you are telling him if it is not supported with relevant detail. The detail may alert him to a point he had missed. But write as briefly as possible.

Now let us deal with down-organisation communication. Consider this memo:

Memorandum from managing director to all staff.
From Monday 3 June, the canteen has been designated a smoke-free zone. All staff will desist from lighting cigarettes until they are out of the canteen.

Leaving aside the merits of this potentially contentious decision, is this the right way to announce it to staff? Certainly not. The boss is the boss, but he should not sound like a Gradgrind. While the employee should be tactful in his communication with the boss, the boss should be diplomatic when dealing with staff. The following memo would achieve better results:

Memorandum from managing director to all staff.
The no smoking policy will be introduced into the canteen on Monday 3 June. From this date, you will be requested not to smoke during meal breaks for the health and comfort of all diners. There is, of course, no objection to lighting cigarettes outside the canteen.

This memo introduces exactly the same policy, but in a less abrasive way. The phrase "requested not to smoke" is less likely to make smokers" hackles rise than the curt "desist from lighting cigarettes". Nobody doubts that a request from the boss is an order, but they prefer to be asked than told. The memo gives a reason for the smoking ban – "the health and comfort of all diners". And it tries, at least, to mollify smoking hard-liners by dressing up the existing policy which allows smoking outside the canteen as a concession.

What points does the down-organisation communicator need to bear in mind?

First, to treat the reader with respect. Even though you may be writing a communication to a person of lesser standing in your organisation or outside, that fact should not show through in the tone you use.

Secondly, give reasons for decisions. All people are more likely to accept a decision when they know the reason for it.

Thirdly, use the language of consensus rather than of command. Orders are for the army (and a few other disciplined services.) They now have little place in for-profit and non-profit organisations that depend for their success on team working.

Fourthly, make sure your communication is clear. Ambiguity and obscurity will confuse people. They will not be certain what you want them to do. Even worse, persistently confusing communications will undermine their confidence in your leadership role.

In and out, up and down – at the end of the day, it is all about dealing with people effectively. The same kind of skills in human relationships that you would use in personal contact are just as valuable when writing to people.

CHAPTER 4

PUTTING ON THE STYLE

THE STRATEGY OF STYLE

There are many aspects to style, some of which concern the technical use of English. But the most important concern the *purpose* of style. The central point about style in business writing is that it is part of getting what you want. We have already seen that business writing is about achieving a purpose. Style helps you do that.

You cannot underestimate the importance of style. The style is likely to have as much influence on your reader as on what you say. It is a human fact that people are driven by both their hearts and their heads, in varying proportions depending on the person. Your style wins (or repels) their hearts and your facts and arguments their heads. Don't imagine that a superb presentation of facts and arguments will overcome major deficiencies in style. Although people are influenced by style and content, style makes its impact first. It either clears the ways for the content or it slams the door.

So is there a "right" style for business writing? Unfortunately not. You must match style to the circumstances of your communication. What is the relationship between the writer and the reader(s)? (See the previous chapter.) What do you want to achieve with the communication? What style will best help you achieve it? In other words the strategy of your business communication and the style are inextricably mixed.

To understand the point, consider this example. You are a shopfitter who has equipped a new store for a client. Now the client is quibbling about a cost over-run on the contract, which you know was quite reasonable. If you give the client the requested £3,000 discount, he will give you a contract to fit his store in the adjacent town. If you refuse, the contract may go to another company, but you might still win it because you know your client was delighted with the quality of your work. Ideally, you would charge the £3,000 and get the new contract, but we do not live in an ideal world. A previous exchange of letters has failed to resolve the problem. It is crunch time.

If you want to be certain of the £3,000 but uncertain of the new contract, the core of your letter could read like this:

A We explained the reasons for the cost over-run at the time they occurred and you agreed that there was no alternative if the job was to be finished to the agreed specification. Under the terms of our contract, we have no alternative but to insist on payment of the £3,000 by the due date. We will, of course, provide a quotation for your new store. In the light of the experience gained on the present contract, we are confident that the problems of cost over-run can be removed in future.

If you want to be hopeful of the £3,000 but certain of the new contract, the core of your letter could read like this:

B John Smith, our contracts manager, discussed the reason for these cost over-runs with Mr Brown, your surveyor, on the site at the time the problem occurred. Mr Brown agreed that the extra expenses were reasonable and said he would recommend payment. In the light of the satisfaction you have expressed with the finished job, we hope that you will now be able to pay the additional £3,000. Mr Smith has already discussed with Mr Brown ways to ensure that no cost over-run occurs in the new contract. We are, of course, delighted that you want us to quote for this contract and the relevant documents will be with you within the next few days.

Both of these letters adopt a style which aims to achieve a given objective. If you have pitched the style right, the subtext of each letter should be clear to the recipient.

Letter A is saying: we've discussed this long enough. The facts are quite clear and you agree them. Now we want our money, but we want to stay friends. We will carry out the new contract if you pay the money.

The subtext of letter B is this: we discussed the problem with you at every stage and you agreed with the extra payments. We think it is fair that you should pay the money and given the quality we provide, which you'll find it difficult to get elsewhere, it would be in your interests to do so. In any event, we'll go ahead with the new contract on an agreed price.

What are the elements of style that signal these different subtexts?

Tone: on a scale of unfriendly, neutral, friendly, the first letter is neutral/unfriendly. The second letter is neutral/friendly. It is a little warmer in tone, signalled by a phrase such as "we hope that you will now be able to pay". A puts it much more bluntly: "we have no alternative but to insist on payment".

Vocabulary: the choice of key words sends signals. In the first letter you have "explained" the reason for the cost. In the second, you "discussed" it. "Explained" brooks no other point of view, "discussed" implies a two-way exchange.

Personalisation: the first letter is impersonal. The corporate "we" is used throughout. In the second, individuals are introduced to give the story a more human face.

Warmth: In the first letter you will "provide" a quotation, a cold term. In the second letter, you will be "delighted" to do so, a much warmer and more enthusiastic approach.

What conclusions can we draw from this exploration of the strategy of style?

First, style is intimately interwoven with what you want to achieve. Style is much more than a way of putting a literary gloss on your business writing. You use style as a weapon to get what you want.

Secondly, the style changes the character and the nature of the message. You use style to implant a subtext in your message which reinforces your position to your reader. If you were talking to a person, your body language would give out messages as well as words. In business writing, style takes part of the role of body language.

Thirdly, there are a number of elements – such as tone, vocabulary, personalisation and warmth – which can be used to create a style that serves your purpose. You should be aware of them and how to use them to achieve your objectives.

Fourthly, style is a business policy. In the example we have just looked at, the style you choose depends on the result you want. That is a business decision which needs to be taken by those responsible.

Develop your writing styles

You may need to write a wide range of different kinds of communications. You need to adapt your style to suit each kind. Is your writing style set in concrete, or can you match it to the moment? One problem is that too many business people think it is hard enough to develop any writing style, let alone several.

However, it is possible to adopt a more flexible approach to your business writing if you take on board one lesson: writing is a business skill that can be learned like any other. When it comes down to it, the act of writing is about 20% inspiration, 40% technique and 40% persistence. Don't worry too much about the inspiration at this stage – that will come with time. (In fact, you probably have more than you realise.)

Instead, concentrate on the technique and the persistence. In the end, technique boils down to a skill at using the building blocks of writing – words, grammar, punctuation. So you reckon your grammar is poor (you never were very good at parsing sentences at school). No need to worry about that. The kind of skills you need as a business writer are practical not academic. You can acquire them in a similar way to learning a spreadsheet. Indeed, if you have a blind spot about business writing, it may even help to start thinking about writing as using language as a business tool, for that is exactly what you should be doing.

We shall return to the question of technique later in this and subsequent chapters. What about persistence? It is possible for all business people to acquire writing skills, but that does not mean they will use them successfully. Skill is about potential and persistence realises that potential. No sizeable writing task is ever successfully completed without persistence. First, you need persistence to practise your new found writing skills, to polish and hone them to greater heights. Secondly, you need to apply persistence when you undertake any writing assignment. Persistence means sticking at the job to get it done, not accepting second best, making sure the document you produce is completely fit for purpose, checking, redrafting, refining and polishing until you are satisfied.

Does every writing job require that level of persistence? Possibly not. But every writing task requires some persistence. And a major writing assignment calls for solid application often for very long hours.

Using style as a weapon

We have seen that writing skill is 40% technique. One of the most important techniques is the ability to adapt your writing style to the task in hand. You will find a number of different styles useful to you in business life. One problem in coming to grips with this topic, is that style can be subtly moulded into an infinite number of varieties. However, there are a few common styles which are at the heart of 80 per cent of business writing. So let us explore some of the more commonly used writing styles:

Leadership style: you use this style when you are the leader and want to convey the fact. Compare these two examples:

A *Letter to shareholders from chairman*
The results for the last financial year have just been published and they report an increase in profit of 30%. Despite this, our market is under increasing pressure from foreign competition. As a result of this, it would probably be most unwise to sanction an increase in the level of dividend.

B *Letter to shareholders from chairman*

I am pleased to report an increase in profit of 30% for the last financial year. But in the year ahead we face increased foreign competition. As a result, I cannot sanction an increase in the level of dividend.

In which version does the chairman sound like a leader? Clearly, B. These are the techniques that make him (and can make you) sound like a leader.

- Write simple sentences. B has three sentences of 16, 10 and 13 words, A three sentences of 20, 11 and 20 words, 12 words more than the leader's version. Leaders get straight to the point.
- Say it hard. A softens the bad news ("our market is under increasing pressure"). B puts it on the line ("we face increased foreign competition").
- Don't qualify. A prevaricates: it would "probably be most unwise" to increase the dividend. B leaves no doubt: "I cannot sanction an increase…".
- Display confidence. "I am pleased to report…" in B sounds more positive than the neutral first sentence in A which gives no clue as to the chairman's feelings about the results.

You should use the leadership style when you are in a position to make policy, express opinions and set the pace for your organisation.

Soft soap style: you use this style when you want to lower the temperature, keep things calm, avoid stirring up a row. Consider these examples.

A Memorandum to the Post Room manager

I have discovered that you sent the invitations for the sales presentation by second class post. You should know by now that these always go first. Kindly take steps to ensure that this does not happen again.

B Memorandum to the Post Room manager

It appears that a batch of invitations to the sales presentation were despatched by second class post. It is established company policy that these should be mailed by first class post. It would be helpful if procedures could be introduced to ensure that company policy is implemented in this respect.

Version B sounds a good deal less direct than version A, but that is the point. Perhaps the writer has good reasons for not wanting to provoke an argument with the post room manager. The two versions reveal some lessons about the soft soap style:

- Remove personalities. The "I" and the "you" in the first sentence of version A immediately personalise the problem. Version B gets round that problem by discussing the problem neutrally in the third person – "it appears".
- Use the passive voice. Because the passive voice is a more indirect way of writing ("invitations… were despatched" in B) it sounds less aggressive than the active voice ("you sent the invitations").
- Don't call your reader a fool. A suggests the post room manager "should know by now" that sales invitations go out by first class post. He probably does know. It might have been a mistake. B states company policy as a means of establishing what should

be done in future in a non-controversial way without pointing the finger of blame or implying incompetence.

- Use a longer word. As a general rule, you should use a short word when it will do, but short words can explode like bombs in a sentence ("you sent" in A reads like accusation and is one). "Despatched" in B is a softer word and makes the error seem less of a problem.
- Don't issue orders. When you want something done by somebody who is not in your direct line of command, make a suggestion rather than issuing an order. The last sentence of B sounds wordy (and is meant to) but is less likely to irritate the post room manager than the final sentence of A.

You should use the soft soap style when you are writing about controversial or negative issues to an equal or a superior.

The "corporate we" style. This is the organisation's version of the "royal we". It is the linguistic equivalent of collective responsibility. Consider these examples:

A I have received an answer to your complaint from the despatch department. I have contacted them and they claim that although your order was received on Friday, the following Monday was a bank holiday. As they do not work on bank holidays, they could not send out your order until Tuesday. I feel sure they would wish me to pass on their apologies for any inconvenience caused.

B We have examined your complaint. The reason for the delay was because your order was received in the Friday before a bank holiday Monday. Because the office is closed on bank holidays, it was not possible to despatch your order until Tuesday. We apologise for the delay in sending your order.

At first reading, A sounds an acceptable reply. But is the writer endorsing what the despatch department says, reporting it, or implying criticism of the department. B solves that problem. This is a complaint to the company and the company as a whole is accepting responsibility for it. In using the "corporate we" style:

- Give a unified view. Don't report the views of one part of the company as though there may be an alternative. One company, one voice.
- Speak for the company. You are not writing with your opinion but providing information about the company's activities or views. Your writing should reflect that, even if your own views differ.
- Accept responsibility. In A "they do not work" on bank holidays. In B "we do not". Even worse, the final apology of A shuffles off responsibility in a way likely to damage the standing of the despatch department in the eyes of the customer.

The "corporate we" style is also useful when you are writing a document which involves incorporating information from one or more other people. It ensures that the document is read as the collective views of the company or department that initiated it rather than the personal opinions of the writer. This is true even for letters signed by individuals.

Committee-speak style: you use this style when you want to report events and decisions in a completely neutral way. Consider these examples:

A Committee minute: Park closing time.

Mrs Jones, who is involved with the local residents' association, had written in to complain about "nocturnal larrikins" in the park. Apparently, the local youngsters get up to "all sorts". Quite a few of the people round the table agreed. Most of us think the problem could be sorted by keeping youngsters out of the park at night.

B Committee minute: Park closing time.

The committee had before it a letter from Mrs Jones, the chairperson of the Residents' Association. The letter referred to the nuisance caused to local residents by young people using the park late at night. The committee felt that leaving the park open in the evening could result in it being used for undesirable activities.

Accordingly, the committee RECOMMENDS:

That the park gates be closed from 8.00pm to 7.00am.

Version A is certainly more colourful, but B is more business-like. Perhaps committee minutes should be more lively, but they are written for two main reasons – to describe the consideration of business and record the passing of decisions and recommendations. In using the committee-speak style you should:

- Speak for the body rather than the individuals. You are reporting the considerations of a corporate body (in this case, a committee, but in other instances, a working party, planning group, etc.) Your writing should reflect the views of the group as a whole, except where individuals' views are especially reported.

- Write impersonally. Refer to yourself and your colleagues only as a corporate body or individually in the third person. You do not want your readers to be diverted by your differences of opinion, but by the conclusions your group as a whole has reached.
- Be precise. A talks about a letter received from Mrs Jones, who is "involved with" the local residents' association. B makes it clear she is the chairperson.
- Spell out what action you want. A talks vaguely about keeping youngsters "out of the park at night". B makes a concrete recommendation. It separates the recommendation from the rest of the text to focus readers' attention on it.

You should use this style for working party reports, committee minutes, and any other document conveying information to an audience of people where the writer's personal opinions should not be apparent to the readers.

Colourful style. Just as there are cases when you need to keep your style flat and neutral, there are others when you want to make it colourful and lively. Look at these two examples:

A Invitation to an opening
An invitation is extended to attend the official opening of the Furniture Happy Mart on Thursday 2 May at which the ceremony is to be performed by Mr Thomas Tickle, the television personality. After the ceremony, it will be possible to view the products available in the store. Refreshments will be served.

B Invitation to an opening
Please, please come to our mega-opening ceremony. The

venue: the new Furniture Happy Mart. The date: Thursday 2 May. Don't be late. Tommy Tickle, the hilarious compere of TV's top game show, Tickle Your Fancy, will declare the store open… in his own inimitable way. There will be champagne and lots of yummy snacks. And plenty of opportunity to buy. Our Mart is an Aladdin's Cave of luxury three piece suites at unbeatable prices.

In version A, the opening sounds about as much fun as a funeral. Indeed, the invitation is couched in terms almost designed to put you off attending. B makes the opening sound as though it might be fun. So lessons for the colourful style are:

- Keep sentences and words short. Short sentences make for livelier writing. While there are many opportunities for using a long sentence, such a method of writing requires the reader's close attention, and can impede understanding by forcing the reader to disentangle the different ideas from one sentence, a problem he might not have had if those ideas had been expressed in several sentences. See?
- Use words which grab attention. Mega-opening might not be the Queen's English but it wins the reader's attention in the first sentence of B.
- Use more adjectives. Adjectives are describing words. They add excitement to the ideas expressed. So the compere is "hilarious" and the snacks are "yummy". But don't go too overboard with adjectives. Otherwise, the pace of your writing will slow down and begin to sound tedious.
- Use a metaphor. A metaphor is when you say something is something else. In B: "Our Mart is an Aladdin's Cave…" Or

you could make it a simile, by saying that something is like something else: "Our Mart is like an Aladdin's Cave…"

- Be specific. Saying exactly what you mean always sounds more interesting than a generalisation. "Champagne and yummy snacks" sounds much more appealing than "refreshments will be served".

If you can master the strategy of style you will find that your writing makes a quantum leap in effectiveness. It seems obvious that you should adapt your style to the circumstances. Yet there are other factors which influence business writing style… often not for the best.

Chapter 5

Tactics for effective writing

Why am I writing this rubbish?

George Orwell wrote a celebrated essay on language and politics. In it, he pointed out that the way we use language is increasingly influenced by what we believe – in fact, by politics. Because business is also deeply influenced by management or office politics, the same kinds of problems that Orwell originally identified now afflict much business writing.

Examples are not hard to find. An organisation doesn't become smaller but is "down-sized". It doesn't sub-contract, it "outsources". Workers are not told they're sacked. Instead, they're given "positive counselling prior to outplacement". It is very easy, from a writer's point of view, to say that this kind of language should not be used in business writing. Such language is not always used out of laziness, lack of skill or because the writer does not know better. On the contrary, he often knows only too well the dangers of using plain speaking to describe potentially explosive situations. Instead, the language is used deliberately to soften a blow, obscure an unpleasant fact, divert attention from a damaging situation.

Does this mean the use of plain English is dead in business writing? Not necessarily. First, there are plenty of opportunities in business writing where "politics" does not intrude. There is no excuse for not writing in plain English in those cases. The trouble is that the weavers of political business English set a bad example. Their obscurantist vocabulary and tautological phrasing catches hold. Unless, of course, you make a positive effort to ignore it. So the first lesson is to resist the influence of bad business English.

Secondly, there is the issue of what to do if you feel political pressures in your organisation forcing you into using unacceptable business-speak. The first question you should ask yourself is this: is it really necessary for me to write like this? Will using plain English make solving the underlying problem easier or more difficult? Frankly, it is hard to see how using straightforward language can make solving a problem more difficult. Indeed, using plain language can be a necessary pre-condition of communicating the real nature of a problem to those affected by it. "Political English" is designed to obscure meaning, to camouflage intentions.

The next question to ask is whether your use of language treats your reader with respect. Bluntly, are you using weasel words and phrases because you are trying to get away with something or even put one over on him? If this is your intention, perhaps you should carry on writing the way you do. But you may not retain much respect among other business people.

If it is not your intention, why are you doing it? Perhaps you think it makes you sound more important. "The year-end fiscal out-turn was commensurate with our fourth quarter budgetary projections," sounds important. It means, "we made as much money as we predicted three months ago," a more homely mixture of words which is easier to understand. But before you go for the pre-fabricated phrases, ask yourself: which would I rather read? In the end, the user of self-important English is rather like the person who puts on white-tie and tails for a "come as you are" party. He may think he looks important, but the other guests are laughing at him behind his back.

If you find yourself dropping into the constipated style of the worst of business English, there is one simple question you should ask yourself. Why am I writing this rubbish? If you decide there are overwhelming business reasons for writing: "the negative feedback detailed in the market research overview from the established customer base necessitates an immediate reappraisal of the short-term manufacturing plan with immediate effect," you must, regrettably, do so. Otherwise, just write, "because our customers don't like it, we better stop making it."

The core of good style

If you have eschewed "political" business English, what other points should you bear in mind in order to improve your business writing? We have already seen that the style you choose varies from one kind of communication to another and is driven by what you are trying to achieve. But beyond the strategy of style, lie a number of tactics:

Write briefly. Writing and reading are hard work, so why do more of them than necessary? A large number of business documents are longer than they need be. The reason: their authors have not thought out their writing task before starting it. It is all too easy to scribble away and continue scribbling until you have said everything. You will not, however, have said it as succinctly as you might have done. Because it is not succinct, it will be less readable. Because it is less readable, it will be less effective in achieving your purpose.

George Bernard Shaw once ended a letter to a friend: "I'm sorry this is such a long letter. I didn't have time to write a short one." Paradoxically, writing short often takes longer than writing long. It also takes more skill. Short writing involves these steps:

1 Think out what you plan to write.

2 Plan how you will write it.

3 Choose the most appropriate format.

4 Make each point succinctly.

5 Read what you have written.

6 Decide how you can make it shorter without losing any essential information.

7 Revise your text.

8 Go back to step 5 and go through steps 6 and 7 again.

9 Complete your document when you are confident it needs no further revision.

The major reason for over-long documents is wrong structure. Because the structure is wrong, information is not necessarily being presented in the most effective order. As a result, the writer is forced into repetitions and digressions. Lesson: right structure is the mother of brevity.

The father of brevity is good sentence construction. The key point here is the construction of the sentence rather than whether the sentence is long or short. On the whole, you should prefer shorter to longer sentences. But a document that reads well varies the length of the sentences. There are three main points to bear in mind about sentence construction:

1. *Sentences written in the active voice are shorter and clearer than sentences written in the passive voice.* It is easier to understand what is happening in the active voice. Active: "I sent the report to John" (six words). Passive: "The report was sent by me to John" (eight words).

2. *Avoid verbal ballast.* Read a significant number of reports and you will find a lot of words doing no work but making up the

volume. The phrases are not hard to spot:

It seems to me...
It should be noted that...
It is worth making the point that...

There are are plenty of others. They increase the number of words without adding meaning, so should be avoided.

A special kind of verbal ballast is tautology – saying the same thing twice:

These new low prices are the result of reductions.

New low prices have obviously been reduced.

Finally, there is a rich undergrowth of words that are often used, but rarely need to be.

The factory has moved to the new site precisely because it is more accessible..."

Precisely? This word is often used for emphasis when no emphasis is needed. The sentence makes its point just as well without "precisely".

Your report was really useful...

Really? Another word used for padding. Again, the sentence works better without it.

3. *Use short words rather than long words.* Long words often sound more important, but they don't always convey meaning as effectively. "Additional expenditure" sounds grander than "more spending" and uses nine more letters, but it doesn't say any more. Besides, a sentence made up of short words is often easier to understand than a string of long words. Winston Churchill may have coined the phrase "terminological inexactitude" for the short word "lie" but when he wanted a power sentence he chose short words: "I have nothing to offer but blood, sweat, toil and tears."

If you write briefly you will have made an excellent start in your effort to write clearly. It is easier to grasp the main point of a document written in 500 words than one written in a thousand. It also saves the recipient two or three minutes reading time. Writing briefly forces you to be clear, because sentences which obstruct understanding stand out more clearly in a shorter document.

One reason why people write at length is that they want to emphasise an issue they regard as important. They think that pouring more words on to the point makes it stand out more. But it is like tipping rubbish on top of a slag heap. The pile becomes bigger, but obscures the view. In other words, length is the enemy of emphasis. Consider these examples:

A It cannot be stated too strongly that if the present circumstances are allowed to continue there is no question that the company will fail to make a profit in the current fiscal period.
B At present, the company is heading for a loss this financial year.

In A, the writer has tried to build up the significance of what he is saying with phrases such as "cannot be stated too strongly" and "there is no question". But he only succeeds in delaying the real message from the reader – that the company will make a loss. In B, the writer puts the message up-front. It explodes on the page in front of the reader.

Apart from writing briefly, there are other techniques you can use to make your writing as clear as possible.

Be direct. Don't hedge your sentences around with "ifs" and "maybes" which only muddle the reader:

A It is just possible, providing our components are delivered on time and if there is no exceptional absenteeism in the factory, that we will be able to complete the order on schedule, but there is also the possibility that the production manager will want another order to take precedence.

What is the reader to make of this? Will the order be completed on time or not? A clearer version is B.

B The order will be completed on schedule subject to timely delivery of components and no extra absenteeism. The production manager makes final decisions about work schedules.

It is easier to see what is happening here. The order will be completed on time, depending on three other factors. The reader can see what those factors are and what impact they might have on an on-time order.

A further writing fault which obstructs direct prose is the excessive use of "qualifiers", words like "rather", "pretty" and "little".

For example:

> It is rather pleasing to report that the pretty big effort of the management team ensured the project was a little under budget.

There is a sentence bringing some good news, except that the sentence is weakened by qualifiers. It is much stronger when it reads:

> It is pleasing to report that the big effort of the management team ensured the project was under budget.

As Strunk and White say in *The Elements of Style*, qualifiers are "the leeches that infest the pond of prose, sucking the blood of words."

Be precise. The reader can only understand what you tell him. If you write vaguely he will understand vaguely. There are many ways to be vague, but vagueness comes in two main varieties:

1. *Casual use of words.* Consider this example:

> Thank you for coming to see me the other day. I would very much like to think in terms of you joining us but I feel we need to get together again to hammer out details.

The lucky reader of this letter will wonder whether he is or isn't being offered a job. He might also be puzzled about the need to "get together again". This version clears up all the problems.

Thank you for coming for an interview on 19 September. I would like to offer you the post of secretary with this company. However, before finalising details of my offer, I would like to have a further meeting with you to discuss salary and employment benefits. I would be grateful if you could attend another meeting on 27 September at 3.00pm at this office.

This version is longer, but at least it makes clear what is going on.

2. *Imprecise use of facts.* Consider this example:

I am not happy about the service we are receiving from your company. Several deliveries were late last week and some were also short. We have also had cases of the wrong products being delivered to the wrong depots…

Clearly, all is not well. But the unlucky recipient of this letter will not be able to start putting it right, until he knows a little more about what is going on. Certainly, there are facts in the letter – "several deliveries were late", "wrong products were delivered". But the facts are not specific enough. What has happened here is that the writer was too lazy to get the information together to write a precise letter, thus:

I am not happy about the service we are receiving from the distribution division of your company. Orders numbered B298 and R367, due for delivery on 7 October, were not delivered until 11 October. Furthermore, order R367 was delivered wrongly to the Chigwell depot instead of to Raynes Park.

This letter provides the facts the recipient needs in order to investigate the complaint. It is more satisfactory for the writer, too. He is more likely to get a prompt and helpful response to his complaint.

Be unambiguous. The problem with ambiguity is that you think you mean one thing and your reader thinks you mean something else – or is not sure what you mean. Some ambiguity is caused by careless sentence construction. For example:

> You write: "Could you let me know by the end of the week whether you will be able to deliver our order?"
>
> You meant: "Could you let me know whether you will be able to deliver our order by the end of the week?"

Result: no order but a friendly phone call on Friday afternoon to let you know the order will be delivered next week.

The remedy for this problem is to check every sentence for meaning at revision stage (see chapter 8). You might also create ambiguity when you use words in a special way which is not understood by your reader. Every trade and profession has dozens, sometimes hundreds of these words in its own special jargon. For example:

> We have a large ethical business.

To an ordinary reader, this might suggest the company is run to the highest business standards. But if the letter came from a pharmaceutical business, it would indicate the company supplied a lot of drugs available on prescription – "ethical" has a special meaning to pharmacists.

A final ambiguity problem we should consider is that of word substitution – what writers call the "elegant variation". Consider this example:

The price of our X2000 computer is £500 and the X3000 system is £750. Alternatively, you may prefer the X4000 machine at £900.

Here, the writer has used the elegant variations "system" and "machine" instead of computer. Yet nothing is gained by this, except possibly some mystification by the reader. He may wonder whether a "system" includes extra elements which a "computer" does not. The message: refer to the same thing by the same word if you wish to avoid ambiguity.

Be complete. You will leave your reader puzzled if you do not include all the information he needs to understand what you are saying. Here are some examples of incomplete writing:

All despatch work is handled at our Preston depot.

Problem: there are at least 18 Prestons in the United Kingdom (plus 20 Preston-somethings). The reader does not know which one you mean. Solution: with places or buildings always give enough information to identify it exactly.

The working party considered the effect of ACT on DCF in the light of the ZBB policy.

Problem: if this is one accountant writing to another, the reader may know that ACT is advance corporation tax, DCF discounted cash flow and ZBB zero base budgeting. Even so, he might need to cudgel his brains unnecessarily to recall the acronyms. A lay reader will be complete baffled. Solution: always write an abbreviation fully the first time it is used, even for readers you think will understand it. Keep writing it out fully if it is a lay reader, but use the acronyms for a reader with the same knowledge as you. Exceptions: those organisations and concepts better known by their initials than their full title such as BBC and VAT.

> There will be a discount for exceeding our minimum order within a month and a further discount for prompt payment.

Problem: the facts are missing. How much is the discount and the minimum order? Solution: a clearer version would read:

> There will be a 5% discount for exceeding an order of £500 within a month and further 2½% discount for payment within 30 days.

Always put in the exact facts so that the reader knows what you mean.

Be reader friendly. It is possible to obey all the rules mentioned above and yet still produce a piece of writing which the reader finds difficult to digest. Perhaps the reader finds it "hard work" reading what you have written. Even though you are not writing for entertainment, it pays to write in a way which helps your reader understand what you have to say. In being reader friendly, you need to consider two main points:

1. *Put the emphasis where it counts.* In anything you write, there will be points you want to ram home and information that is

subsidiary. You need to give the important points more weight in the way you write. For example:

We acknowledge your order arrived late and we have given you a £10 refund.

This is weak partly because the negative information – the late delivery – is first in the sentence and partly because both halves of the sentence, either side of the "and" have equal weight. A stronger version is:

We have given you a £10 refund to compensate for late delivery.

There are several reasons why this version works better. The positive news comes first. The sentence is not divided into two halves. The refund is linked more closely in the reader's eye to the late delivery – the words "to compensate" perform that task. An alternative way of recasting the sentence is:

Because your order arrived late, we have given you a £10 discount.

In this sentence, the notion of cause and effect is introduced. Cause: late delivery. Effect: £10 discount. Using cause and effect links ideas logically together in the reader's mind and helps him to understand what is happening.

2. *Make ideas flow in sequence.* Sometimes writers string information together without considering the way in which one idea links to another. As a result, the reader is left to consider what

seem to be a lot of disjointed pieces of information. Consider this
example:

> The components were not delivered until Wednesday. The
> factory started to assemble them on Thursday. The first order
> was despatched on Monday. The final order will not be sent
> until the end of the month.

A clear cycle of events is taking place here, but the writer is
not helping the reader to make a judgement about them. The
writer has not thought out how the presentation of these ideas can
help to achieve his purpose. For example, this could be part of the
factory manager's report to the production director. It could read
like this:

> Because the components were not delivered until Wednesday,
> the factory could not start to assemble them until Thursday. As
> a result, the first order was despatched on Monday but the final
> order will not be sent until the end of the month.

In this version, ideas are linked together. Cause and effect (see
above) is introduced to the first sentence. The phrase "as a result"
links the information in the second sentence to the first. The writer
uses the "but" in the second sentence to colour the production
director's view of how the orders are going. However, if the factory
manager was writing to a customer, he might draft it like this:

> The factory started assembly work on Thursday even though
> the components were not delivered until Wednesday. Despite
> this, the first order was despatched on Monday and the final

order will be sent by the end of the month.

In this version, the factory manager gives the customer a more positive view of events. The positive news is in the first part of the first sentence. The "even though" emphasises how quickly the factory started to assemble the components once it had received them. In the second sentence "despite this" again emphasises the positive aspect of delivering the orders despite the difficulties.

Final faults

If you follow the points mentioned here, you will eliminate many of the possible areas of fault in your writing. There are a few other miscellaneous problems you need to be aware of:

Clichés. You should avoid clichés like the plague (although this sentence hasn't). Because clichés are tired and second rate their excessive use can give your writing the same flavour. Clichés are a substitute for thought. They can also make the reader feel you don't mean what you write:

I have explored every avenue to find the model you need.

The cliché leaves the reader with the impression that perhaps the writer hasn't bothered.

I have telephoned all of our branches to find the model you need.

That says what the writer has done, sounds sincere and avoids the cliché.

Slang. Using slang usually reduces your status in the mind of your reader. You may think that slang makes your writing sound informal, even friendly. Too often, it just cheapens what you have to say. For example:

> Because the budget is spot on I have given the project the thumbs up.

This simply does not sound right, and the reader may wonder about the judgement of the writer.

> Because the budget is acceptable, I have asked for the project to proceed.

This sounds more formal but sets the right kind of tone for a business communication about an important topic.

Chapter 6

Words on a page

Pleasing to the eye

When it comes to business writing, appearances are not deceptive. If you open a document and are faced with page after page of text with hardly a break, it looks boring. It probably is boring. Even more important, the writer has not organised the information in his text to make it appealing to you.

When you write a document – whether a one paragraph letter or a 500-page report – if the words don't look good on the page, your reader starts with a disadvantage. So do you. For it will be that much harder to get your ideas across. That is one reason why it is important to think about the appearance of your document. Creating a satisfying and effective appearance is part of the writing process.

There is another reason. Thinking about the appearance of your document – the physical structure of it – helps you to organise your ideas. If your thoughts pour onto the page in a stream of consciousness, the reader is unlikely to see which are your main points. If you organise your ideas visually on the page, the reader can immediately see what you are saying.

Power of the paragraph

At school you may have been taught that a paragraph is a unit of thought, usually with a "topic sentence" at the start which sums up the subject of the paragraph. That is not a bad starting point for business writing, but it does not go far enough. The paragraph helps you to parcel up your ideas so you can deliver them to your reader one by one.

Another reason for the paragraph is to help your reader get through the document. The end of a paragraph provides a natural break point in your writing – and in the reading. It is a signal to the reader that you are about to move on to another topic. This means that as far as possible, you should try to follow the "unit of thought" rule. If you break a paragraph in the middle of an idea, you risk confusing your reader.

What happens if the idea is too big to be written about in one paragraph? Then you have to split it into more than one paragraph. There is no fixed length to a paragraph but if one runs on for, say, more than half a page, it starts to look too long. You will often find that if this happens, you are writing about more than one idea. Look for the natural break points in what you are saying.

A final point: do not underestimate the extra impact you will gain by organising your document into well thought out paragraphs.

Wide open spaces

After paragraphs the next point to consider is how the words look on the page. There is among some writers a mentality that believes that every part of the page should be filled with writing. Often such documents come from the office Scrooge whose passions in life include not "wasting" paper and bending paperclips back into shape so they can be reused. Not wasting paper is a commendable aim, but you *will* waste paper when your document contains words which do not effectively communicate.

Your words will communicate more effectively if you give them room to breath on the page. If your are writing a report-style document some points to consider are these:

Top and bottom: leave some white space at the top and bottom of each page. On an A4 page, about one inch at the top and one and half inches at the bottom is about right. It makes the page seem less heavy to the reader.

Margins: you should leave reasonable margins at each side of the page – again about one inch is often right. But in some documents where you want each point to stand out, it may be effective to leave even more than one inch.

Space between paragraphs: in a book, paragraphs usually run on without any space between them. In a business report (and sometimes a letter) it is often more effective to leave a line space between each paragraph. The space helps to give a visual structure to the information. Where this style is used, the first line of a new paragraph is not indented. The line space has already done the visual job the indent would provide. The same style is increasingly favoured for business letters, although many organisations still prefer to run on paragraphs without leaving a line space, but indenting the first line of each.

Variable indents: indenting some paragraphs more than others provides visual variety. It also helps to create structure on the information. You may find variable indents useful when you are numbering paragraphs (see below). But a word of warning. You should avoid having too many different line width measures in your document – normally not more than three. The aim of variable indenting is to help you improve the clarity of information – for example, by indenting lists or examples – so the indenting structure should be logical and make sense to the reader. If the reader cannot understand why a paragraph is indented, there may be something wrong with your approach.

A question of emphasis

How can you emphasise information in your document? There are a number of devices, but they should be used with care. The main way of delivering emphasis is in the style you use to write. Typographical emphases should not be used as a fig leaf to cover poor writing.

Another danger is that emphasis methods are used too often, which reduces their impact, or that too many different kinds of emphasis are used close to one another, which confuses the reader. These points are illustrated in what follows.

Methods of emphasis include:

Capital letters. Normally capitals should be restricted to the start of a sentence or proper nouns. Capitals can add emphasis when used with restraint. The main use for capitals is in headings. They rarely work well in the body of the text of a document. A common misuse of capitals is in company and product names. You may think you ram home your company name by always mentioning it in capitals:

I am writing with details of products provided by ACME SERVICES LTD.

This is just about acceptable, but looks slightly amateurish. To the reader, the capitals look like the typographical equivalent of an inferiority complex. The following works better:

I am writing with details of products provided by Acme Services Ltd.

Underlining. This is an effective way of giving emphasis to some words and phrases – but do not use it too often. The correct use of underlining is:

- Headings: to give the heading extra weight on the page.
- Titles and names: underlining can be used as a replacement for italics to pick out book or report titles or the names of ships, etc. For example:

A The Economy of Europe was out of stock, but I am including the Economy of America and the report Sales of Machinery in South America 1985-1990 with this letter.

B The <u>Economy of Europe</u> was out of stock, but I am including the <u>Economy of America</u> and the report <u>Sales of Machinery in South America 1985-1990</u> with this letter.

In these two examples, B is much clearer than A because the underlining separates the titles from the rest of the words in the sentence. Equally effective is to put the titles into italics.

Headline news
One way to help readers find their way through a document is through the skilful use of headings. You will find them particularly useful in a report, but could also use them in a letter. For example, a customer writes asking about progress on three separate orders. You will set out the information he needs in three main paragraphs. If you give each of the paragraphs a heading, your customer will be able to see at a glance that you have provided all the information he needs.

There are two main kinds of headings – those which deal with subject matter and those which describe the structure of the document. Headings which describe structure are simple and often one word – for example, introduction, purpose, objectives, summary, recommendations. These headings help your reader to find the different kinds of information he is looking for. For example, he may want to glance quickly at your recommendations before reading the whole document. That is difficult unless he can find them quickly.

Subject headings deal with the content and are often longer. Even though a heading is just a few words, there is still a skill in writing it. Points to consider are:

Keep the heading brief. Headings are best written in a kind of telegramese. For example:

A A report which examines the impact of the new opening hours on staff working practices.

This is too long. The reader has to discard too many words to get at the meaning. B is better:

B New Opening Hours: Impact on Staff Working

There is no need to say that it is a report in the title. The reader is intelligent enough to see that.

Make headings informative. Brevity is important, but not at the expense of information. Consider these examples:

A Summary of the Chancellor's Budget Proposals
B Effect of Budget on Business Plan

Both have the same number of words, but the first is too general to give a clear idea of what the report is really about. The reader might think the report is just a general overview of the Budget. The second heading gives a clearer indication of the scope of the report. The heading describes the report's purpose. The message here is that you should always try to encapsulate the main purpose of the document in the heading.

Numbers that count

When is it useful to use numbered paragraphs in a document – and what rules should you follow? In most cases, you need to use numbers when you are writing a longer document, such as a report. But there is also a case for using numbers in some shorter letters and memoranda.

You can decide when to use numbers by considering the purpose they perform. There are two main purposes. First, they are an attention grabber. The numbers show your reader the points he must consider. Take this example:

A You will get several benefits from our product. It is fully guaranteed for up to a year. We also provide an extended warranty up to five years. On top of that, the product comes in a choice of seven colours. There will be a 10% discount on orders of more that five units.

B You will receive four main benefits from our product:
1. One year's guarantee
2. Five year extended warranty.
3. Choice of seven colours.
4. 10% discount on orders of more than 5 units.

Version A provides all the information, but the writer has presented each benefit in a slightly different way. As a result, the reader has to work at understanding what they are. In B, the benefits are numbered and clearly identified. The reader can see at a glance what he is getting for his money.

The second purpose of numbering is for reference. This is particularly important for longer reports where it is easier to cite part of a report by the numbers of its paragraphs than by describing their content.

In a simple case, the numbering convention you adopt is as easy as one, two, three. But in some documents, you will find the numbering rather more complex. In choosing a numbering system for a document you have two main choices:

1. *A mixed numbers and letters system.*

With this approach your main sections are numbered 1,2,3 and so on, paragraphs with a,b,c and sub-paragraphs with Roman numerals – i, ii, iii. This approach can be shown in outline in this example:

1 Greengrocery
  a Vegetables
    i Potatoes
    ii Carrots
    iii Peas
  b Fruit
    i Apples
    ii Oranges
    iii Pears

2. A decimal numbers system.

With this approach, the main sections are numbered with primary numbers, paragraphs move to the first decimal place and sub-paragraphs to a second decimal place. Using the decimal system the greengrocery example, looks like this:

1.0 Greengrocery
    1.1 Vegetables
        1.1.1 Potatoes
        1.1.2 Carrots
        1.1.3 Peas
    1.2 Fruit
        1.2.1 Apples
        1.2.2 Oranges
        1.2.3 Pears

Both systems have their uses and their protagonists. In some ways the first approach is more user-friendly because the number-letter-number hierarchy is easy to follow. However, it becomes unwieldy if you need to have a large number of paragraphs and sub-paragraphs within each section. Once you reach the second half of the alphabet in paragraphs, you begin to lose track of how many paragraphs there are. The other drawback is the use of Roman numerals which beyond a point become more difficult to follow – did you immediately know that xviii is 18?

The decimal approach has all the severe logic of mathematics behind it – and some of the drawbacks. You can begin to see one of them in the greengrocery example. All those decimal points start to make the non-mathematical mind boggle. You may also find that it is surprisingly easy to become muddled when you are numbering paragraphs at three different levels. ("Now should that be 5.6.5 or 5.5.6?")

Whichever approach you decide to adopt, you should keep two simple rules in mind. First, be consistent throughout your document. Secondly, have a maximum of three levels to your numbering system as more levels confuse rather than clarify.

Get a little list

Effective business writing means using words in the best format for conveying your meaning. Sometimes you will find that a list or a table can improve the clarity of what you write and save a lot of words as well. Consider the next examples:

A The branches in Luton, Norwich and Northampton will be closed. The branches in Peterborough, Ipswich, Southend, Faversham and Dover will be expanded. The branches in Oxford, Reading, Slough, Newbury and Gloucester will be reviewed in six month's time.

B Branch status is as follows:
To be closed:
    Luton
    Norwich
    Northampton
To be expanded:
    Peterborough
    Ipswich
    Southend
    Faversham
    Dover

To be reviewed in six months:

Oxford

Reading

Slough

Newbury

Gloucester.

Both A and B contain the same information, but the list in B makes the information clearer on the page. It also removes the need to write three similar boring sentences one after the other.

A list becomes even more useful when it turns into a table, which is essentially a series of coordinated lists. Consider this example:

A Several members of staff will be involved in completing the contract and each will have a timescale. Ted Jones, in the body shop will have to ensure that all units are sprayed. Tom Brown, in warehousing will have to make sure the units are packed. Meg Smith in despatch must send out the order to the customer by 20th May. In order to do this, Tom will have to complete the packing by the 18th which means that Ted must finish the paint spraying by 14th.

In this paragraph, the three people mentioned must search, among the words to find out what they have to do. Now look at an alternative way of presenting the same information:

B CONTRACT COMPLETION

Department	Task	Responsibility	Deadline
Body Shop	Paint spraying	Ted Jones	May 14
Warehouse	Packing	Tom Brown	May 18
Despatch	Posting	Meg Smith	May 20

This is much clearer. Moreover, because the information is presented logically and clearly, it looks as though the job has been organised sensibly. Every person involved can see at a glance what he or she has to do and by when. Moreover, the tabular approach describes the tasks in a logical sequence which the text version does not.

Tables, such as this, are greatly under-used in business writing. They add value to information for the reader by displaying it more clearly and by showing the relationships between different parts of the information. You will also find that putting information in a table helps you as a writer to establish that you have thought out what you want to say logically and that every piece of information you need to convey is included.

CHAPTER 7

SUBJUNCTIVES, SEMICOLONS AND STUFF

GRAMMAR AND COMMON SENSE

It may seem strange to you that a book about business writing should leave grammar almost to the end. Does this mean that grammar is not really important? Certainly not. Grammar is as important to understanding language as driving on the left is to avoiding traffic accidents.

On the other hand, there is no need to become a grammar freak. It is possible to write well without understanding some of the more obscure rules of grammar, just as it is possible to drive a car without understanding what goes on underneath the bonnet. However, there may be a few occasions when you are perplexed about a point, it does help to understand a few formal rules of grammar. For example, should you write:

A None of us is able to attend the annual general meeting.

B None of us are able to attend the annual general meeting.

Which is correct? One school of thought argues that because "none" is a contraction of "not one", it must be followed by a singular verb. So A is the correct version. On the other hand, that unimpeachable grammatical authority *Fowler's Modern English Usage* explicitly states that it is a "mistake" to assume that none is singular only. And the Oxford English Dictionary says that the plural construction is more common.

See how complex fine points of grammar can become. You can end up losing sight of the main issue, which is to write clear and persuasive English.

The "none" example shows that, with grammar, there is not always a "right" answer. However, in most cases there are. Whoops! That should read "in most cases there is". The verb in the sentence is governed by "answer" which, in this context, is "understood".

What you need as a business writer are a few guidelines with which to judge questions of grammar:

Be kind to the Queen's English. Grammar is an aid to understanding, so it is foolish to ignore it as though it weren't important. Precision is often important in business English and you use grammar to engrave an exact meaning into a sentence.

Keep a sense of proportion. On the other hand, you do not want to become obsessed by grammar. Grammar is a tool of language, like words and punctuation. A good workman cares for his tools, but recognises that they are less important than what he makes with them.

Ignore language superstitions. These include supposed rules which nobody has ever followed, such as never beginning a sentence with "and" or "but". Such superstitions mostly seem to emanate from ageing school teachers, who have, themselves, forgotten where they first learnt them.

In any event, good writing is largely a question of having an ear for the language rather than an exhaustive knowledge of the rules of grammar. Perhaps you already have a good ear for English in which case a sentence that is grammatically incorrect will sound wrong:

Five per cent of the staff could be cut from each branch and yet still be able to handle the same amount of business.

You can just feel something is wrong with that sentence, even if you cannot immediately put your finger on what it is. When a sentence sounds as though it might be wrong, you need to look more closely at its meaning. What does this sentence mean? It is saying that the five per cent of staff cut from the branch (rather than the 95 per cent left) will be able to handle the same amount of business. What it wants to say is that the branch will be able to handle the same amount of business, after a five per cent staff cut. The sentence needs to be recast:

Each branch could sustain a five per cent staff cut and yet still handle the same amount of business.

What should you do if you do not have a good ear for language? You must try to develop one. Listen more closely when good English is spoken. Try to grasp the essential simplicity that lies behind the construction of a sentence which is easy to understand. Make a conscious effort to eliminate any common faults you know you have, such as using double negatives – "we don't need none" instead of "we don't need any". In time, perhaps quite quickly, you will find you develop a natural feel for the correct use of English.

Avoiding common mistakes

Even writers with a good grasp of grammar occasionally make a slip. And some slips are more common than others. In business English the worst slips are those which obscure or even change the meaning of what you intended to write. Eight of the most common mistakes in the use of business English are:

1. *The roving pronoun.* When using a pronoun, make sure the reader understands to which noun it refers.

Mr Brown has discussed the paperwork with Mr Smith and he will deal with it.

Who is dealing with the paperwork? Is it Mr Brown or Mr Smith? The pronoun "he" could refer to either of them. If Mr Brown is dealing with the paperwork, the sentence needs to be recast like this:

Mr Brown has discussed the paperwork with Mr Smith and will deal with it.

If Mr Smith is dealing with the paperwork the sentence should read like this:

Mr Brown has discussed the paperwork with Mr Smith who will deal with it.

2. *The disappearing subject.* Make sure you remember what the subject of your sentence is, right through to the end, especially if the sentence is a long one.

The budget report shows sales are falling and has not improved since the beginning of the year.

Here the singular verb "has" can only refer to the "budget report". So the sentence is saying that the budget has not improved since the beginning of the year. What the writer is trying to say is that sales have not improved since the beginning of the year. The verb should be "have" to agree with "sales". The sentence should read:

The budget report shows sales are falling and have not improved since the beginning of the year.

3. *Word order confusion.* When you write a sentence take care to put the words in the correct order. Writing too hastily or with insufficient thought can result in some embarrassing gaffes:

The managing director was asked to deal with petty theft in the office by the board of directors.

Dear, dear. Here is word order confusion that could lead to a libel writ. It is, hopefully, not the directors who are responsible for petty theft in the office. The sentence should read:

The managing director was asked by the board of directors to deal with petty theft in the office.

4. *The Is don't have it.* I and me cause common confusion. I is used when it is the subject of the sentence, me when it is the object. So this is wrong:

Mr Snipe and me will be going to the trade exhibition.

So is this:

The French delegation will meet Mr Snipe and I at the trade exhibition.

In the first sentence, "me" is part of the subject of the sentence, so you should write:

Mr Snipe and I will be going to the trade exhibition.

In the second, old Snipey and you are the object of the sentence. It should read:

The French delegation will meet Mr Snipe and me at the trade exhibition.

5. *Sentence fusion.* Every sentence should end with a full stop. The careless writer runs two sentences together separating them by an inadequate comma.

The committee decided that the next meeting should be held a week later than normal, this was so the chairman could attend after returning from holiday.

As is often the case with sentence fusion, this is nearly one sentence. Dropping the words "this was" would fuse the two sentences acceptably into one:

The committee decided the next meeting should be held a week later than normal so the chairman could attend after returning from holiday.

If "this was" is retained, the sentence needs a full stop after "normal".

6. *Never the twain.* The opposite of linking together two related but separate sentences, is the grammatically right but stylistically wrong joining together of two different ideas which should never have met between the same full stops.

The cargo of bananas has arrived from Honduras and the second phase of the office development in Dagenham is well under way.

This incongruity occurs when the writer hasn't thought out in advance what he wants to say or how to say it. Alternatively, the writer is racing along, pouring out information without thought to structure. It causes confusion because the reader is left wondering whether there really is a connection between a cargo of bananas from Honduras and the office development in Dagenham. Both ideas need separate sentences and probably separate paragraphs.

7. *Aberrant apostrophes.* According to writer Keith Waterhouse, who coined the phrase, these are one of the curses of today's writers. (There's an apostrophe used correctly – and another.) An apostrophe is used correctly to denote the possessive (when something belongs to something or somebody else) or to produce a colloquial contraction (such as don't for do not). The following sentence contains several common examples of aberrant apostrophes:

The 1990's are the year's in which several businesses will feel the recessions effect on their sales" figures.

The sentence also contains a missing apostrophe. It should read:

The 1990s are the years in which several businesses will feel the recession's effect on their sales figures.

8. *Word confusion.* Unfortunately, the English language abounds with similar words which are often confused for one another. In a worst case, the result is a sentence like this:

The principle affect of to many enquiries is to make there sales system impractical.

There are five word confusions in this sentence:

- "Principle" (fundamental truth) should be "principal" (first in importance).
- "Affect" (verb meaning "to produce an effect on") should be "effect" (result or consequence).
- "To" (preposition meaning "in the direction of") should be "too" (adverb meaning "more than wanted").
- "There" (adverb meaning "in or at that place") should be "their" (possessive pronoun meaning "belonging to them").
- "Impractical" (meaning "not something that can be done") should be "impracticable" (meaning "not workable").

So the sentence should read:

The principal effect of too many enquiries is to make their sales system impracticable.

What can you do if you suffer from word confusion? First, list the words you find confusing side by side – such as affect or effect. Then look up their meaning in the dictionary. Work at understanding the different meanings of each. Finally, practise at using them in sentences.

This chapter is called "Subjunctives, Semicolons and Stuff." So far, neither subjunctives nor semicolons have been mentioned. Indeed, both are largely becoming relics of grammatical history. Today, the most common everyday English use of the subjunctive is to denote a hypothetical state:

If I were you.

The subjunctive may also be heard on most football terraces on Saturday afternoons in such expressions as:

Clear off, ref.

However, in business English, it is not a topic that need detain us for long.

The semicolon, much beloved of eighteenth century novelists, is on the way out, too. It is *not* a slightly stronger version of a comma, and should strictly be used only to separate parallel expressions in the same sentence:

The delivery of the sub-assemblies on Tuesday morning, three weeks late; the poor service received from your company over the past year; the failure to provide any adequate explanation; all these lead me to conclude we should end our business relationship.

This is the correct use of the semicolon, but in a piece of

business English it looks faintly absurd.

Which brings us to the final point. While forms like the subjunctive and semicolon decay, new words and new grammatical forms are born. The English language is a living organism, changing all the time, sometimes for better, sometimes for worse.

CHAPTER 8

ANY OTHER BUSINESS

PARETO PENMANSHIP

Picture this scene. A committee or working party is finalising the draft of a report. Suddenly, a member of the committee fixes on one sentence. It reads:

A study of working practices in the factory revealed that materials waste could be cut by 17%.

"That won't do," says the committee-man. "The word 'revealed' suggests we were hiding the fact. We should write 'showed'."

"A poor choice of word," says another. "If we say 'demonstrated' it sounds more positive."

"I disagree," says a third. "The best word is 'suggested' because we can't be certain it would happen in all parts of the factory."

An argument ensues. Tempers flare, accusations fly, dictionaries are brandished. Nobody stops to ask whether it really matters what word is used or whether there are more important parts of the report to which the committee should devote its attention.

You have probably encountered situations like this. They demonstrate that in writing, as in many other business activities, the Pareto Principle applies: 80% of your effort should be devoted to what really matters and only 20% to the linguisitic spit and polish that makes a piece of writing shine.

So what does really matter? Two things above all:

1. *Making sure the document serves the purpose for which it is intended.* Before you start to write, you need to ask (as we have seen in chapter one) what the purpose of the document is. It may be a lengthy report on developing a new product or a short letter replying to a simple customer query. Whichever is the case, you should ask yourself four questions:

- Does the document provide all the information the reader will need?
- Is the information presented in a logical way?
- Is the writing clear and unambiguous?
- Is the writing pitched at the correct level for the reader(s)?

2. *Making sure the document helps you achieve your objectives.* In other words, your document has to be persuasive. You should ask yourself six more questions:

- Have I selected the most appropriate facts and marshalled them in the most effective way?
- Should I include any more examples to reinforce my points?
- Does the structure of the document lead the reader towards the conclusion I want?
- Does my choice of language steer the reader towards the conclusion I want?
- Have I clearly stated the action I want?
- Is there any superfluous material in the document which clouds the main points and could reasonably be excluded?

If the answer to any of these questions is no, your document requires some revision.

Revising with a purpose

To revise a document effectively, you need to go through several stages.

First, read through the document, to get a feel for it as a whole. Did the document give you the message you were trying to impart? If not, why? Is it because the document is too thin in content? Are there important facts or examples missing which ought to be included? Did you spend enough time on gathering together the material you needed to write the document, or do you need to collect more information?

If you find the document is not giving the message you want, or not giving it strongly enough, you need to look closely at the content and structure of the document. One reason may be that the document simply does not contain the hard facts and figures to be convincing. Another is that the facts and figures are included but are not presented in an effective way.

If you find either of these faults, your first priority is to put them right. You may need to redraft the whole document or parts of it. But do not start until you are convinced you understand where the fault lies and how to put it right. Collect all the extra information you need before you start to redraft. Make sure that you have clearly mapped out a structure that will be effective before you start rewriting.

If, however, you are happy with the general message given by the document, you can move on to the next step.

In the second stage of the revision process, you read through the document again more slowly. This time you are looking to make sure that each section hangs together logically and that there are adequate links, where needed, from one section to another. In the second read-through you will be asking yourself different kinds of questions. Is the document correctly paragraphed? Are headings and sub-headings used where they can be helpful? Are the sentences of different lengths to vary the pace for the reader? Are there any points where the writing is not clear?

If you discover faults as a result of asking these questions, you should try to put them right as you work through the document. Providing that none of them involve major restructuring, they should not alter the overall flow of your document.

The third and final part of the revision process is a check through for spelling errors, punctuation slips or grammatical solecisms. It is also important to check your document for consistency. For example, do you give distances in miles in one part of the document and kilometres in another? Where a word has alternative spellings (enquiry or inquiry, for example) have you consistently used one throughout?

When you have completed these three revision processes, you can sign off your document, confident that you have done your best.

Advice from the great

Be clear about this: business writing is not about literary writing. It is about effective communication. But all writing is hard work. As Samuel Johnson said: "What is written without effort is in general read without pleasure." The Roman poet Horace summed up what you have to achieve in business writing as in any other: "You will have written exceptionally well if, by the skilful arrangement of your words, you have made an ordinary idea seem original."

But there are dangers even in good writing, according to the British poet Walter Savage Landor: "Clear writers, like clear fountains, do not seem so deep as they are; the turbid look the most profound."

Finally some elegantly expressed advice from Alexander Pope:

True ease in writing comes from art, not chance,
As those move easiest who have learn'd to dance.
'Tis not enough no harshness gives offence,
The sound must seem an echo to the sense.

PART 2

THE PERFECT REPORT

CHAPTER I

THE PURPOSE OF THE REPORT

WHAT IS A REPORT?

In the world of business writing the term "report" has a special kind of aura that other documents don't. The word "report" on the cover page of a document immediately invests the contents with a special authority. For a report implies that the contents are the product of careful research, mature thought and measured expression. In companies, public bodies and voluntary organisations people take decisions, sometimes important decisions affecting the lives of people or the expenditure of millions, based on the contents of reports. When they have to consider an issue they will often call for a report. The contents of the report will colour their judgement of the matter under consideration and influence their decision. In short, the report is a very special piece of work-related writing which has a status far removed from other business writing, such as letters and memoranda.

The dictionary definition of a report tells only half the story. A report is "a formal statement of the results of an investigation, or of any matter on which definite information is required, made by some body or person required to do so." *(Shorter Oxford English Dictionary)*. It is what the dictionary definition implies, rather than what it says directly, that is important for the report writer. It suggests that the report is an especially careful piece of work in which facts have been meticulously collected, opinions considered in a balanced way, and conclusions reported in a sober but unambiguous language.

Of course, not all reports carry equal weight. There are large reports (such as some of those produced by House of Commons Select Committees) and small reports (such as the couple of paragraphs a manager might draft in answer to a simple query). There are mightily influential reports (such as the Beveridge Report of 1944 which mapped out the structure of the modern welfare state) and reports that don't receive a second thought (such as a product faults summary received by managers in a US manufacturing company which always showed zero in every column – because the company no longer made the products). There are reports assembled as the result of the work of a team of people over a long period of time (such as the report of an investigation into a major accident) and reports penned by an individual in a couple of hours (such as a large number of simple management reports turned out in companies every day). The report is not an animal but a species.

Like other species, members of the report family have the same characteristics:

A clear purpose. A report is normally commissioned with a clear aim in mind. However, the purpose could be one of several. We return to this point below.

A methodical approach. A report approaches its subject matter in a logical and methodical way. There is no "right" way to structure a report, but normally a report could include any or all of the following: an introduction that states the purpose of the report, a section that describes how the report writer or writers went about their business, a description of the evidence collected, a summary of the findings, and a set of recommendations. All these will normally be presented in a sequential way, one following logically upon the other. There are other features which could also appear in some reports and which we will address later.

A special tone of language. Because a report has a purpose, the language used in it is chosen to suit that purpose. Generally, a report is written in language which engages the report's readers at a level they are likely to find appropriate. There is no one writing style that is appropriate to every kind of report. For example, a report of the investigation into a factory death would be written in sober terms and would not be expected to carry any flashes of humour. But a report based on a survey of people's weekend leisure activities could be written with a lighter touch and might contain some well judged sparks of humour. Whatever writing style is chosen, the language of a report should be clear and unambiguous. It should also seek to engage the reader and, where appropriate, win him round to the writer's point of view. We shall return to the subject of report language in more depth later in this book.

As we have seen, the report is a species rather than a single animal. It can range from a single-sided document at one end of the scale to a multi-volumed publication with thousands of pages, perhaps the result of a government investigation, at the other. In between come the bulk of reports – perhaps a dozen pages long, perhaps as many as a couple of hundred pages. It is these reports in between, rather than the two extremes of the single-sided or the multi-volumed, that we are chiefly concerned with in this book. They account for a large proportion of all reports written.

The first point to consider is the different purposes which a report might have.

Defining a report's purpose

Every report is written for a particular reason. So, in that sense, every report has a unique purpose and it is essential that you, as the writer, understand the precise purpose before you embark on the research, compilation and writing of the report. However, while every report has a unique purpose, it is possible to categorise general areas of purpose into which most reports fall. Understanding these different purposes helps your report writing by providing an understanding and framework in which you can approach each unique task.

There are seven main purposes about which you should be aware.

1. *To provide information.* In a sense, all reports provide information but, as we shall see below, the purpose of some reports goes beyond that of straightforward information delivery. There is a specific category of report, however, whose purpose is only information provision.

Consider, for example, a progress report on a new building project. There could, in fact, be several different types of progress report for different managers involved in various aspects of the project. One of those could be a progress report designed for staff not involved in the day-to-day management of the project. This is the report which has as its primary purpose the provision of information. Its aim is to do no more than make people who are interested in what is happening, aware of what is happening. The report is saying simply: "Here is some information that we think you ought to know."

In preparing this kind of report, you should define the purpose of the report by asking these questions:

- How much detail should be included in the report?
- Is the information in the report cleared for general

circulation?
- Who will receive the report?
- What value will the information be to the readers?
- At what level should the information be pitched?
- Is this a one-off report?
- Will the report be filed for reference or thrown away after reading?

2. *To provide a record.* The main purpose of this kind of report is to record information that may need to be accessed at some stage in the future. The minutes of a meeting is an example of a report whose purpose is partly to provide a record of information, which may include decisions taken. However, there are many other cases where a report is compiled solely for the purpose of recording information. Sometimes, such a report will be written only for the writer's own files. Alternatively, it might be circulated to other readers.

Often, the purpose of a report "for the record" is to provide a contemporaneous account of information collected or decisions taken. The report is always there as an *aide-memoire* should the writer or any other reader want to refer to it in the future. Should the subject of the report ever be raised again, the report stands as a (theoretically) incontestable record of what happened. If there is a dispute about facts or about action taken, the writer of the report can say: "Look, this report was written at the time when the information was fresh in everybody's mind."

There is sometimes an element of self-preservation about reports written for the record, especially when they languish in the writer's own files. The report lies there as evidence that information was properly collected, opinions were properly considered, decisions were properly taken, should there be a dispute in the future. Not surprisingly, therefore, such reports are most common in public bodies, where decisions can become the subject of public debate and may have to be defended months or even years after they were taken. However, they are also to be found in commercial bodies.

Take, for example, a situation where a member of staff has been disciplined. The manager responsible for the disciplinary procedures will write a report at the end of the process detailing what was said and what was done. However, that report will not be circulated widely, although it may be sent to one or two other managers involved in the disciplinary process. It is written chiefly for the record – in case there should be any need to take further disciplinary action against the same individual in the future. Indeed, such a report has potentially important significance in any legal action that might arise from future disciplinary proceedings.

In writing any report for the record, you should ask these questions.

- Why is it important to record this information now?
- Who might want to refer to this information in the future?
- Why might people want to refer to this information in the future?
- Is the report likely to be used in any legal or quasi-legal proceedings?
- Does the wording of the report need to be approved by any other people?

3. *To answer a specific query.* A considerable number of reports are written in order to provide an answer to a specific question or request for information on a clearly defined topic. In these

cases, the purpose of the report and the audience for it are clear to the writer from the outset. In this kind of report, the "terms of reference" are defined by the person who has asked for the report. (We shall be exploring the nature of terms of reference in more detail in the next chapter.) This is not to say the terms of reference will make it easy for the report writer to research and compile the report.

The terms of reference of this kind of report could suggest a simple report or a lengthy and complex report. An example of a query demanding a comparatively simple report would be: "Provide a report on the profitability over the past 12 months of our Birmingham branch." Depending on the amount of detail requested, this would be a comparatively simple report to compile. A query demanding a much more complex report would be something like: "Provide a report on the feasibility of opening a chain of branches for our company in the US." In order to produce a report that satisfied this need, the writer would need to consider a large number of different issues. Whereas the first report might take only a couple of pages and not much more than an hour or two to compile, the second report could take a team of people weeks, even months, and might run to a hundred or more pages.

In writing a report to answer a single query, you should ask these questions:

- Is the query (the terms of reference) framed in a way that is clear and unambiguous?
- Is it clear what kind of report the recipient wants?
- What level of knowledge does the report's recipient have about the topic to be dealt with in the report?
- What use will the recipient make of the report?

• What is the deadline for delivering the report?

4. *To recommend a decision.* This is the kind of report which is produced when a board of directors, group of managers or people running a public body want some advice about how to approach a particular decision. Like the reports already mentioned, this kind of report involves collecting information. But the writer or writers (and any people who put their name to the report) will be expected to consider a range of options about the issue under consideration. The report writers will be judged on the quality of recommendations as much as on the comprehensiveness of the information contained in the report. Normally, people called on to produce this kind of report are experts in the subject matter (although this is not always the case).

Reports used to recommend decisions are used in both the public and private sector. Central government, for instance, often sets up bodies charged with compiling a report and making recommendations on various areas of public concern. A "green paper" is a report produced by a government department that explores a range of options about a topic. By contrast, a "white paper" says what the government plans to do. Reports that recommend decisions are also common in local government where an agenda item for a committee meeting will often be accompanied by a report from officers recommending a course of action to the committee.

Similarly, in the private sector, a manager or management committee may be charged with investigating a course of action and making recommendations either to the board of directors or other group of managers.

In writing a report to recommend a decision, you should ask

these questions:

- What is the context of the recommendation the report will make?
- Will the report's recipients require one recommendation or a choice of options?
- Who should be involved in discussing the recommendation?
- What evidence will be needed to support the recommendation?
- In what timescale will the recommendation be needed?
- Have the effects of implementing the recommendation been fully considered?

5. *To influence opinion.* The purpose of this kind of report is to win over people to a particular point of view. Generally speaking, such a report will be produced for wide circulation. On rare occasions, such a report will be on sale in bookshops – for example, "think tanks", such as Demos and the Institute for Public Policy Research, regularly produce reports designed to influence public opinion or the direction of government policy. In most instances, this kind of report is produced by a voluntary organisation or public sector body that wants to win opinion-formers to its point of view. However, in some cases an opinion-forming report is produced by a commercial organisation or trade body that wants to put its point of view to a wider audience.

Because the purpose of the report is to influence opinions, the report writer has to pay great attention to the quality of research and the accuracy of the facts mentioned in the report, as obvious omissions or inaccurate facts will undermine the report's credibility. Opponents of the organisation's point of view will be looking for ways to discredit the report.

Another important point is the quality of the argument. If the report aims to form opinions among a knowledgeable section of the community, the way the report writer constructs his case will be crucial. Readers will expect the argument to be connected together with logical links and supported with valid and illuminating examples. But people's opinions are also driven by their emotions, so subject matter and presentation which appeals to the heart as well as the head may also be effective.

The presentation of a report such as this will also be important. In most cases, readers will not be obliged to read the report as a manager would with a business report that landed on his desk. Instead, potential readers must be enticed into reading the report. Producing the report in an attractive and readable format is one way to encourage readership. Giving it an appealing, even provocative title, is another way.

If you have to write a report to influence people's opinions, you should consider these points:

- Which people is the report seeking to influence?
- What is their current opinion?
- Why are we seeking to change their opinions?
- What are our strongest arguments and how can they be put over most effectively?
- How should we deal with hostile points of view?
- What information should the report contain and at what level of detail?
- In what other ways can the report be made more influential?

6. *To gain publicity.* The purpose of this kind of report is to raise

the profile of the organisation that produces it. It can be similar to the previous kind of report (which can be used to generate publicity) but is also different in some important respects. Several of those kinds of reports can be used to generate media coverage, but there is a category of report whose sole purpose is to produce publicity. Sometimes, this kind of report is produced when the organisation finds it difficult to generate publicity in other ways. Often such a report contains the results of a survey.

Consider, for example, a company that wants to publicise some of the services it provides. Perhaps it sells life assurance policies. It conducts a survey of the different policies held by people and what they think of them. It asks questions about why people invest in life assurance policies and the value they believe they get from them. It probes a range of potentially controversial issues, such as what people think should be done to improve the service provided by life assurance companies. Then the results are presented with an interpretive commentary in a report. Providing the survey has been conducted in an authoritative way, some newspapers and magazines will regard the results of the survey in the report as a worthy news item.

If you are asked to produce a report in order to gain publicity, you should ask the following questions:

- Why do we wish to gain publicity for the subject of this report?
- How will the publicity help our organisation?
- Will the report actually produce positive publicity or could there be negative spin-off?
- Is the content of the report genuinely newsworthy?
- Which kinds of news organisations are most likely to publicise

the report?

- How can the presentation of the report make it more newsworthy?

7. *To meet a statutory obligation.* Many reports are produced because the law says they must be produced. For example, a company's annual report and accounts is produced to meet a statutory requirement. A significant proportion of the contents of an annual report are specified by law, although publicly quoted companies often include a considerable amount of other material in their annual reports. Many public bodies are also required to produce statutory reports. For example, local councils are obliged to submit a range of reports to different government departments.

In producing a report of this kind, the writer must make certain that all the information specified by law is included in the report – and that the information is provided in the way decreed by the regulations. Clearly, this is a specialised task and the writers of such reports will generally be experts in their fields and familiar with the legal requirements.

One problem that sometimes arises with statutory reports is how to include non-statutory information alongside that demanded by the law. In some cases, there is a clash of views between the person responsible for reporting the statutory information and others who might want to give the report a wider appeal. If this happens, it is important that the primary purpose of the report – to meet the statutory requirements – is fully met. There is no reason, however, why some such reports (for example, a company's annual report) should not also seek to achieve broader aims, but these must be carefully defined.

If you are asked to produce a report to meet a statutory

requirement, you should ask these questions:

- Have the statutory requirements of the report been checked with the primary source?
- Has the information been presented in the way required by the body receiving it?
- What other useful information could be included in the report?

A flexible business tool

From what we have seen so far, it is clear that the report is a flexible business tool. (Indeed, a tool that can be used by public sector and voluntary organisations as well.) One danger is that you might think of a report in too narrow a way. It is easy to see how this might happen. You will be familiar with receiving only a limited range of reports in the course of your own work. So your view of the role of the report will be coloured by the reports you receive. You need to adopt a wider view of how you can use different types of report to achieve your objectives.

In skilled hands, the report can be used to achieve many things.

To summarise:

- Understand the characteristics of a report.
- Define the exact purpose of the report you plan to draft.
- Consider the different roles of the report as a business tool.

CHAPTER 2

GETTING STARTED

THE NATURE OF REPORT WRITING

Writing a report is like going on a journey in which there is a beginning and an end but several alternative routes in between. There is no one correct way to write a report because, as we saw in chapter one, there are so many different purposes that the report might have to satisfy. There are, however, a number of different processes that might be involved in writing a specific report. Which ones you use will depend on the exact nature of the report.

Reports fall into two main categories:

- Regular reports.
- One-off reports.

Before considering the processes used in report writing, we should first examine the characteristics of these two types of reports.

Regular reports

Regular reports provide the bulk of the filling for many managers' in-trays. They arrive monthly, weekly, even, in some cases, daily. Most regular reports provide historical performance-related information. For example, a financial report on the previous month, a sales report for the past week, a production report on yesterday's output of the factory. As such, these reports tend to contain mostly financial information, although they may also contain some text commentary on the figures and, indeed, present some of the figures in graphical formats.

If you are made responsible for producing a regular report such as this, you will inherit a set of processes for producing it. The sources of the information to be included in the report should already be clearly identified. The information should arrive according to an agreed timetable. It will be your job to take that information and present it in the report which you produce to an agreed format.

However, if you are asked to take on responsibility for producing a regular report (or if you have been producing one for some time) it might be worth asking a few fundamental questions about the report.

First, why was this report originally produced? Many organisations have reports that have been produced for so long that people have forgotten why they were first wanted. The original purpose of the report is lost in the mists of time. If a regular report has been produced for any length of time – say, more than two years – it is at least worth asking whether the reason for producing the report still exists.

Secondly, does the report still serve any useful purpose? It is possible that the original reason for the report no longer exists, but that it is now used for other purposes. Alternatively, perhaps the report is no longer used at all. There are two ways to find out whether a particular report is still used. One is to ask managers if they still find it useful. Some managers may provide useful feedback, but other managers may not be entirely frank about their use of the report. Another way to test the value of a report is not to send it out or to delay its distribution by a week or two. If nobody rings to ask where it is, you have a good idea of its value.

Thirdly, could the report be changed to make it more useful? If managers are still using the report, but for reasons which have departed somewhat from the original purpose, it is possible that the report could be redesigned to serve the new purpose more effectively. You should ask the people who use the report whether all the information is still relevant, whether the information could be presented in new ways, what new information should be included, and whether the report should appear at the same frequency.

One-off reports

One-off reports are produced for a specific purpose (see chapter 1 for more detail on the possible purposes). If you are asked to produce a report such as this, it might seem that you are starting from scratch. In fact, that might not be the case. It is possible that your organisation has produced a report on a similar topic, which might provide some guidance as to the approach you should adopt.

However, whether that is the case or not, the starting point is to obtain the terms of reference which should define your task. Many of the criticisms of inadequate reports arise because terms of reference were not adequately defined at the outset. So what makes good terms of reference? Consider the boss who says: "Let me have a report on how the new product is doing." What does he mean? If this statement is supposed to be his terms of reference for a report it is deficient in several important respects. In fact, this boss's request does not constitute proper terms of reference at all. Where does it fall short of what is needed?

First, it is not precise. Terms of reference should state exactly what is needed. The phrase "how the new product is doing" could mean anything. Does it mean how the product is selling? Does it refer to the product's reliability? Does it deal with the product's marketing and distribution? It is not clear. Indeed, if there is more than one product, which product is the boss talking about? Secondly, the boss's statement gives no indication of why he needs the information. Does he need the information in order to plan a marketing campaign? Or to review the manufacturing capacity? Or review pricing strategy? Where a report is to be used for a specific purpose, the terms of reference should make clear what the purpose is.

Thirdly, the boss's statement gives no indication of what kind of report is wanted. Does he expect a couple of sheets of paper with basic summary information? Or does he want a 100-page bound briefing book, the result of considerable research? Neither does the statement give any indication of a timescale for the report. When does the manager want the report? Next week? Next month? Tomorrow?

It is vital – not optional – to have full and complete terms of reference before starting work on a report. In order to avoid any confusion, the terms of reference should always be in writing, and signed by the person requesting the report. No doubts, no comebacks. Ideally, terms of reference will include a precise and un-ambiguous statement of the purpose of the report, an indication of why the report is needed, the amount of detail required and a target date for the report's delivery. So, instead of his vague statement, the boss would have issued some terms of reference like this:

"Produce a report on the sales of the new vacuum cleaner in each of our sales regions. The report should:

• show how sales are performing in comparison with the

competition.

- assess the impact of current marketing activities and make suggestions as to how marketing could be improved.
- consider the likely impact of different pricing policies.

The report should be submitted in time to be considered by members of the marketing sub-committee at its meeting on 20 August."

What should you do if you receive terms of reference which are not as complete as this? The answer is to approach the person requesting the report and ask for more precise terms of reference. Make the approach in writing – probably by memo – as a question in writing usually elicits a response in writing. And, as Samuel Goldwyn might have said, a verbal instruction is not worth the paper it's written on.

Reviewing the situation

You have precise terms of reference for a one-off report. What next? You need to consider how you will set about producing the report. In doing this you will need to consider a number of issues including whether you will produce the report alone or as part of a team or working party, what resources you will need in order to produce the report and how you will schedule the work during the time you have to produce the report. We must consider each of these issues in turn.

Alone or together?

The first major issue to consider is whether you will produce the report by yourself or as part of a team. In many cases, that question will effectively be answered for you. If the request is for a report of

modest scope based on information on which you are the acknow-
ledged master, clearly you will produce the report yourself. On the
other hand, the organisation wanting the report may have established a working party or study group and given it terms of reference to produce a report. This approach is common in the public
sector with central and local government bodies, but it is also used
occasionally in the private sector.

There is a middle group of cases where you need to decide
whether you should produce a report by yourself or form your own
working party to do it. Which issues will help you take the best
decision?

First, you need to consider the scope of the information that
must be collected for the report. Can you reasonably get all the
information yourself? Is some of the information outside your own
area of expertise or so specialised it needs an expert? Does some
of the information have to be collected from other parts of the
country or abroad? If the scope of the information you need for
the report is wide, then you should seriously consider forming a
working party.

Secondly, you need to consider whether the report involves
considering significant policy issues. Are they issues that you feel
confident taking decisions about alone? Or would the views of
other people be welcome? Indeed, are the views of others essential
in order to give credibility to the final report? Are there specialist
areas which need to be reviewed by someone with technical
expertise?

If you decide that other people need to be involved in helping
you to produce the report, there are two main ways in which you
can involve them.

1. *You can work with them in a bilateral way.* That is you divide

up the work needed to produce the report into sections. Then you assign each block of work to a different individual. You manage and coordinate the whole project and probably write the finished report from drafts on different sections compiled by the people working on them. If you adopt this approach, you need to consider the following points:

- You must make sure everybody working on the project is aware of the total scope of the project. They should understand how their piece of the jigsaw fits into the whole.
- You should thoroughly brief each individual working on the report on what is expected of him. He should understand what information he is expected to produce, how much detail will be needed, how his information will be used, and the timescale he must work in.
- After each individual has produced his contribution to the report, you should set aside time to discuss it with him. You must make sure you thoroughly understand all the information each person has provided before you issue the final draft of the report. You should ask each person to check for accuracy that part of the report to which he has contributed.

2. *You can set up a working party.* If you adopt this approach you will assemble a group of people to work together in a more formal way in compiling and writing the report. In forming a working party, you need to make sure it is small enough to work effectively but large enough to include all the expertise you need. However, it is not essential to have everybody working on the report as a member of the working party. You can have a core of people on the working party calling, as needed, on the expertise of outside

specialists. But in forming the working party you must ensure that its membership will endow the finished report with the credibility and authority that is needed. This means that every person on the working party should be chosen because he is able to make a measurably effective contribution to the final report.

As the person originally charged with producing the report, you will chair the working party and take ultimate responsibility for the finished report. The working party should only meet in order to progress the work on the project. You should not allow working party meetings to turn into talking shops. This means that each meeting should have a clear aim and agenda. For example, the first meeting will scope the project, identify the work that needs to be completed, set a timetable for each stage of the project and assign responsibility for different parts of the work to specific individuals.

If the report is produced by a working party, there are several other issues that you need to manage. These include how differences of opinion between members of the working party are resolved and how the report is written. These are dealt with in later chapters.

Finding the resources

The next issue you need to consider even before you embark on researching and writing your report is the resources you need to complete the task to a satisfactory standard. For the very simplest of reports, those resources may consist of little more than a writing pad and pen, and a few hours of your own time. But, in reality, a report does not need to become too complex before it requires a significant amount of resources. In producing reports, the use of resources becomes an important issue when you need money, staff time and (possibly) office equipment above and beyond those that you use in your daily work as a matter of course. For example, you may have responsibility for producing a range of regular reports. You will already have the staffing and other resources necessary to do that.

It is when a large project comes along – probably, what we have classified as a "one-off" report – that you need to consider the use of resources more carefully. At a simple level, you can consider the resources you need under three headings – staff time, external resources and general expenses.

Staff time. Producing a report of any significant size is likely to use up considerable amounts of staff time – time which will be diverted from other work. You need to make a judgement about whether you can absorb the amount of time needed in your department's general work, or whether you need a budget for extra staff time. It can be useful to make a rough calculation of the number of days each member of staff is likely to be working on the report. Multiply the number of days by the daily employment cost (salary plus national insurance and other employment expenses, such as office space) to produce an estimate of the cost of staff time needed to produce the report. Then ask the question: does this report justify this expenditure? If you are not sure that it does, it might be worth showing the costs to the manager who has commissioned the report. Perhaps the expense of the report will give him second thoughts or get him to revise his views of the task.

External resources. In the case of a large report, you might need to use different external resources. For example, you may need to engage the services of consultants with special expertise to help you research and compile either parts of the report or the whole report. Typically consultants might be needed for tasks such as:

- Providing technical expertise – for example engineering, financial or legal.
- Conducting surveys – for example, market research or focus group interviews.
- Producing artwork – for example, charts, graphs, maps or special drawings.

Before you begin work on the report, you should assess what external resources are needed and make arrangements to engage them. You should provide a detailed briefing to all external people working on the report. It is also essential to define the work you expect them to do and the timetable in which they should perform it in a written contract, which in simple cases can be a commissioning letter.

General expenses. Again, the level of general expenses can vary dramatically depending on the nature of the report. For a small report, the general expenses are not likely to be much more than the cost of printing and distribution. For larger reports, you could incur a considerable range of general expenses. Categories to consider when drawing up your budget are:

- Report publishing. Can you or your staff complete the work or will you need the help of a design company?
- Report printing. How large will the report be? How many copies will be needed? What sort of binding will be used? (Chapter 6 provides more guidance on this issue.)
- Travelling expenses. Will you or others working on the report need to travel to collect information for it?
- Working party costs. If there is a working party, what about the travelling expenses of members attending meetings as

well as the cost of rooms for meetings?

- Market research/surveys. If you are commissioning these, have the costs been included in the budget?
- Library subscriptions. If the research involves access to specialised libraries, have these costs been included?
- Artwork. Will you need to commission an artist to prepare artwork for charts or drawings and so on or for the front cover?
- General overheads. Are there any other general costs which ought to be included in the budget?

How sophisticated you make the budgeting exercise depends on the size and complexity of the report. For a very small report, there is probably not much point in drawing up a budget. For a medium sized report, a brief note of the main costs should be enough. For a large project, conducted over several weeks or months, you might want to create formal processes in order to build a budget and subsequently to monitor actual costs against that budget. It is worth pointing out that the costs of a large report, involving the work of several senior managers over a period of weeks, could run into several tens of thousands of pounds.

There is another value from the budgeting exercise. Just as there is no free lunch, so there is no free report. If more managers are aware of the costs of producing reports, it will enable them to gain a better grasp of the trade-off between the costs of creating them and the value they provide.

Scheduling the work

In nine cases out of ten – and probably even more often – a report is needed by a specific date. That date may be tomorrow in the case of a small report. It may be in a year's time – even two years time – in the case of a major project. Where you are faced with producing a report for which the amount of work is clear and the subject matter is familiar, you will probably not need to draw up a formal schedule. The way you will handle the work will form up automatically in your mind ("I'll look up the facts on Tuesday, write it on Wednesday, and get it word processed and printed on Thursday").

But for larger reports, this informal approach is unlikely to be adequate either for scoping the project to start with or monitoring its progress as you proceed. This is especially true when the production of the report involves several people and the use of outside resources. In scoping a project, you need to perform three basic tasks, which will vary in complexity depending on the size of the project:

1. List all the different tasks that must be completed in order to produce the report. Each task should involve a self-contained element of the work such as completing interviews, conducting a survey, writing the final draft of the report or printing the report. You should estimate the amount of time needed to complete each task in hours or days and also the elapse time – the length of the period over which those hours or days will be used. For example, a task might take eight days spread over four weeks.

2. Place the tasks on a critical path. You and your team must complete the tasks in a logical order. List the tasks in the order in which you must complete them. You can do this diagrammatically, showing where one task must be completed before another starts and where one task overlaps another.

3. Finally, allocate each task to a specific person or team of people. In some cases, you might be allocating a task to an outside

consultant or specialist supplier. In such cases, you will need to liaise with the specialist to discover how much time he believes he will need to complete the task.

At the end of this process, you should have a written work plan which shows all the tasks in critical path order with start and finish dates and with responsibilities allocated. This will be an important working document as the project proceeds, for it will enable you to keep control of the different tasks. You should regularly monitor the progress of the project against the dates in the work plan.

To summarise:

- Understand the difference between regular and one-off reports.
- Decide whether to produce your report by yourself or as a member of a team.
- Estimate the resources you need to produce the report.
- Schedule the work needed to complete the task.

Chapter 3

Researching a report

Research with purpose

Every report has a purpose. That much we discovered in chapter 1. The skilled researcher directs his research in a way that uncovers the information he needs in order to make his report serve the purpose for which it is intended. This point is important because too many report writers veer to one of two extremes.

One type loves research and immerses himself in it with enthusiasm. Unfortunately, he follows every little byway in the research material he finds with the result that he amasses a huge body of information – too much to produce a well directed report. The other type finds research a bit of a bore. He skates over the most important points and assumes he knows the rest. As a result, he thinks he knows it all (when he doesn't) and is in danger of drawing the wrong conclusions.

If you are a skilled researcher, you will position yourself somewhere between these two extremes. You will direct your research so that you produce material that serves the purpose of the report. You will not become bogged down in unneeded minutiae but you will make sure that you obtain the detail you require to make a convincing case.

Which brings us to another important point about research. Bluntly, is the purpose of your report to relay facts, to discover something previously unknown or to put a point of view? All three will influence the way you approach the research. If you are relaying facts, the main focus of your concern is to find the relevant facts and confirm their accuracy. If you are seeking to discover something previously unknown, you may need to spend quite a lot of time trawling through literature looking for information that is relevant to the subject you are researching. If you are arguing a case, you will not be seeking information in an impartial way, but be looking for evidence that supports your case.

All this boils down to a simple point. When people compile a report there is often a "hidden agenda" – an under-cover purpose to the report – not stated in the formal terms of reference. If there is a hidden agenda for your report, you need to understand what it is and direct your research to fulfil it.

Freshening a regular report

Much of what is said above applies to all reports, but perhaps chiefly to the kinds of reports we have termed "one-offs". As we have seen, a large number of reports are regular, produced with the same categories of information and in the same format on every reporting cycle. On the face of it, research does not play too large a part in these reports. The information comes in from the same sources every reporting period and is massaged into the chosen format of the report.

In fact, even this kind of regular report needs a new research initiative every once in a while. To begin with, such reports become stale. The format chosen, which originally served a useful purpose, becomes out of date. Yet through inertia, it never gets changed. Another problem is that the quality of the information declines. People whose task it is to provide information for regular reports soon learn when they can get away with errors, inaccuracies or inconsistencies. As they creep up this unwelcome learning curve, the value of the information they submit slips down a quality slide.

There are several courses of action you can take with regular reports to make sure they remain useful. First, you should periodically ask the users of the report for their opinion on the report's value. What information in it do they find especially helpful? Which information do they scarcely look at? What do they use the information for? Is there any information not regularly included in the report which they would welcome?

Secondly, you should periodically audit the accuracy and completeness of the raw material information you use in compiling the report. Go back to source and check the accuracy of the information against the primary sources from which it was compiled. Question the compilers of the information about the methodologies they use. This could uncover fundamental flaws in both the nature and quality of information they are submitting.

Finally, examine the way in which you compile the report. Are you presenting the information in the most helpful format? Is the information presented in a way that helps the managers use it to take decisions? Does the report need more or less detail?

It is by adopting this constantly critical approach, rather than just accepting what is there, that a regular report remains a valuable working document rather than another pile of bumph in the in-tray.

Sources of information

The next point to consider is where you will obtain the information you need for your report. With a regular report, this is unlikely to be too much of a problem because (as we have seen) the sources of information are already defined. However, it could be a problem with a one-off report, especially if the report is complex or you are not especially familiar with the subject matter.

Suppose, for example, you are commissioned to produce a report which examines the feasibility of your company moving into a new line of business. By definition, this is a subject about which you will not know much, if anything. It is not like producing a report on, say, the past year's performance of your own department where you are already familiar with much of the information and know where to find the rest of it. Instead, you are moving into uncharted seas, How do you set about the research?

With this, or any other research project, the sources of information you can tap fall into two main categories those within your organisation and those outside it. We shall consider both in turn.

Internal sources of information

Your own organisation is a vast reservoir of information, perhaps a greater information resource than you realise. In a large organisation, you will probably be aware of only a fraction of the main information resources in your company – for example, the information that can be accessed on the internet, the books in the company library, the body of reports and research produced over the years. Beyond your own knowledge lie great oceans of information. In fact, the breadth and depth of information in your organisation is probably much greater than you imagine. We need to consider the potential information sources you can access under a number of headings.

People. This is the primary source of information in your company, arguably the most valuable and almost certainly the most under exploited. Every member of staff is a potential mine of information, not only about his current job responsibilities, but about his previous work experiences. Take the case of researching a new business area. Perhaps there are members of staff who worked in that area in the past and have useful information to provide or who can, at least, point you in the right direction for your research.

. The problem is how to find out which members of staff know what, especially if you work in a large organisation with hundreds or thousands of employees. Your first port of call should be the personnel department. It should retain the CVs of all members of staff who applied for jobs. It may have other records about the specific expertise of employees, such as those who have attended training courses or conferences. Finding those staff members with the knowledge you are looking for could be a lengthy experience, unless the personnel records are computerised and can be searched using keywords. Alternatively, you could put out a call for people with the knowledge you want through a company newsletter, information bulletin or intranet.

In drawing on the knowledge of in-house people, you need to keep a couple of points in mind. First, how recent is their experience? If they have not had any direct contact with their subject for several years, they may be out of touch. Their information and views could be positively misleading rather than helpful. Secondly, at what level were they involved with the subject you are researching? It may be that they were only involved at a junior level but you need a more senior viewpoint. Finally, what opinions do they hold about the subject? You must take care to treat their opinions with caution, They represent only one point of view and there may be other more relevant views to take into account.

Company library. This is an obvious source of information, but only the largest organisations have their own company library. A professional company librarian is familiar not only with research materials in his collection but with other sources of information, He will be able to provide considerable advice on seeking out published sources of information.

If your organisation does not have its own library, it certainly has what you might call informal mini libraries scattered around the offices. Individual managers may have collected books over the years. It is worth contacting some of them to see if they have anything that might be relevant to your research or if they know of any relevant publications.

Databases. Nowadays, vast amounts of information are stored on computers. In the past, most of the information was numerical but now larger amounts of text and graphics are stored on databases. You should find out what databases are available in your organisation and decide whether any of them hold information that could be relevant to your research.

External sources of information

Outside your organisation lie thousands of bodies holding information that could be relevant to a particular research report. Some of the most important categories are:

Public libraries. There has been a revolution in many public libraries in the past decade. No longer are they just dusty repositories for ageing detective stories. Instead, many have built substantial business collections, both in the borrowing and reference sections. Some libraries even offer specialised services, such as copies of company annual reports. The local librarian is helpful and will tell you what research sources are available in his own and nearby libraries.

Customers and suppliers. Both these groups are potential useful sources of information which are frequently overlooked. Of their very nature, both have a wide experience of dealing with different kinds of organisations. In certain circumstances, your contacts within customers or suppliers may be willing to help with information or with tips about where to seek the facts you need.

Trade associations. Most companies and public sector bodies belong to at least one trade association or similar kind of organisation. Such bodies exist partially to be a repository of information about their relevant area. Many maintain their own libraries. Membership frequently provides access to the library. Even if your company is not a member of the association you believe might be able to help in your research, it is still possible you could access its information. Some associations allow outside researchers to use their libraries for a fee. Alternatively, the association's public affairs officer might be willing to help with limited advice to get you started.

Professional associations. As with trade associations, many managers in your organisation will belong to their relevant professional association. Again, the same principles apply. You can seek access to the library of the relevant professional association.

Internet. Undoubtedly, the greatest source of information is now to be found on the internet – specifically, the World Wide Web. No matter how abstruse the subject, it always seems as though there's something somewhere about it on the Web. But a word of warning: not all information on the Web is reliable. Much of it comes from sources that "have an agenda" – they are providing information that supports their point of view rather than seeking to present an objective overview of a subject. So it is important to be aware of the provenance of any information you collect from websites. That said, there are, in most business areas, reliable websites with large amounts of useful information.

Conferences and exhibitions. Most trades and industries have regular conferences and exhibitions which cater for their needs. Attending these can prove a useful source of information. However, you gain the most benefit from an exhibition – especially some of the larger trade shows – if you attend with a clear information-gathering purpose in mind. Most big shows produce good catalogues which provide a guide to the exhibition as well as a useful source of reference afterwards.

Research techniques

At the same time as you are identifying the sources of information you will use in compiling your report, you also need to give some thought to the research techniques you will use. Some of the most common techniques are:

Desk research. This term refers to the systematic sifting of information already published in books, magazines, newspapers and other documents. It is often the essential first step to a research project for it helps to identify the main issues which are important, define the boundaries of the research and uncover sources of further information. As a first phase, desk research also helps you to understand more fully the topic you are researching before you move on to other phases of research, such as interviews or surveys.

If you have not done much desk research before, it might at first seem rather daunting. Where do you start? These tips should help:

• Seek the help of a good librarian in identifying main sources of information about your subject.

- As you identify books that are possibly useful, use the contents and the index to narrow down those which are likely to be of most help.
- As a first step, skim-read material, in order to gain an indication of its relevance. Do not waste time ploughing through long texts of only marginal importance.
- Study the most relevant texts more closely, making notes on or photocopying those sections of particular importance.
- When researching from newspapers and magazines, concentrate initial research on those periodicals that provide a regular index – for example *The Times* and *The Economist.*
- In unindexed periodicals, look for regular topic sections that appear in every issue – for example "new orders', "company news" – that might contain information of relevance rather than ploughing through the whole of every issue.
- Treat desk research as a voyage of discovery rather than a tedious job to complete in the minimum possible time. For example, look closely at the references in relevant books. The referenced works might provide more valuable information than the book you are studying.

Interviews. You could find that you need to obtain information by interview from people in your own organisation or outside it. You can conduct interviews either face to face or over the telephone. In general, telephone interviews work best when you already know the interviewee and the interview is reasonably short – say, less than half an hour. Beyond that length, telephone interviews tend to become trying and increasingly unproductive. However, there are isolated instances when you might want to conduct a longer interview. One case would be if the person you are interviewing is overseas.

For the longer, more complex interview you should always opt for the face to face approach because it is more likely to provide you with insights and detail you may well have missed in a phone interview. In order to get the best from interviewing, you should follow these tips:

- Always understand the purpose of the interview. Be quite clear in your own mind why you want to interview a specific individual and the kind of information you hope to gain from him.

- Brief the interviewee on the purpose of the interview at least a couple of days before it takes place. Preferably, you should brief the interviewee in writing. This will give him time to prepare and assemble any background information he needs before you arrive.

- Prepare a written list of the areas you want to discuss before you go into the interview. This will help you think through the structure you want the interview to take. In some cases, you may actually want to ask a list of specific questions. In others, you might want to talk around specific topics in a more general way.

- Take the interview at a measured pace. Give the interviewee time to catch his breath by engaging in a few pleasantries before you plunge into the formal part of the interview. Move at a business-like pace through the topics you want to cover, but make sure you give your interviewee as much time as he needs to answer each question. Otherwise, you may miss useful detail.

- Decide before you start the interview, whether you are going to make notes or tape-record it. Check with your interviewee that he is happy with whichever option you choose.
- Thank your interviewee for his help at the end of the interview (and it does no harm to send a thank-you letter afterwards if he has been especially helpful). Ask if you can contact him again briefly by phone to check any points that need further clarification.

Questionnaires and surveys. These are an effective means of assembling data when you want to collect information from a fairly large number of people in a structured way. Questionnaires can be useful either to produce factual information (for example, which makes of office equipment do you use?) or opinions (for example, what do you think of different makes of office equipment?). You can conduct questionnaires and surveys by post, telephone, face to face interviews or by e-mail. The method you choose depends on how many people you want to contact, the nature of the questions, and the amount of detail you require in the replies.

The following tips should help when organising a questionnaire or survey:

- Decide on the purpose of the questionnaire. What information are you trying to discover? What use will you put the information to in your report? Is there a better way of obtaining the information you want?
- Decide on the most effective way of conducting the questionnaire – by post, telephone or face to face interviews. Then draw up the questions. Be realistic about both the number of questions you can expect people to answer and the topics

they will be prepared to provide information about. Consider offering a small incentive for completing the questionnaire – such as a summary of the findings.

• If using a postal questionnaire, make the printed form easy to complete and return. Include a postage-paid envelope. Include a short and personalised letter asking the recipient to complete the questionnaire. In the letter, explain why you are conducting the questionnaire. Target questionnaire recipients carefully. Only send questionnaire forms to relevant people. Give a deadline for returning questionnaires.

• If possible, test the draft questionnaire on a small sample of people similar to those who will receive the final version. Use the results of the pilot testing to refocus questions and smooth out ambiguities.

Observation and recording. This category of research covers a spectrum of different activities. At one end is a complex scientific experiment or testing programme, such as that carried out on a new drug by a pharmaceutical company. At the other, is the simple counting of information from a single source – such as counting the number of passengers who get on each train at a railway station.

At the top end of the range, a major experimentation programme requires enormous amounts of "specialised" expertise. However, there are more modest circumstances in which you could be called on to conduct some observation or recording in order to produce information for a report. The following tips should help:

• Understand clearly why you need the information for the report. What role will it play? Do you need information to support a particular point of view? How will the information be presented in the report and at what level of detail?

- Study the feasibility of collecting the information you need. Can the information be collected at a reasonable cost? Is it physically possible to collect the information and over what period of time will you need to deploy the resources?
- Devise the most effective way of collecting information. Will you need to collect information on a tally sheet? Is there any way you can use technology to collect the information more effectively? Test the method you propose to use before you move into the full programme in order to identify any problems.

To summarise:

- Conduct research with your report's ultimate purpose in mind.
- Consider ways to reinvigorate a regular report.
- Identify the sources of internal and external information you can access in research.
- Choose the research technique most appropriate to the task.

Chapter 4

Drawing the right conclusions

Getting organised

As the research for your report proceeds you will accumulate a mass of research material. You need to impose some order on this material rather than allowing it to develop into a muddle. One key to this is the careful filing and cross-referencing of research materials. How complex your filing system is, and how much cross-referencing you decide to do, depends on the size of your project. In a small project, the material you accumulate might well be organised successfully in two or three files, possibly even one. For larger projects a more complex filing system is needed.

You should give some thought to the filling system you will use at the outset of your research. But do not set the filing system in concrete at that stage. Be prepared to change the filing system as your research proceeds to accommodate the nature of the information you are accumulating.

There is no one correct way to organise a filing system for a report research project. But you should consider two possibilities. The first is to organise your research materials by document type. For example, you would create separate files for interview notes, survey results, press cuttings, other companies' literature and so on. Obviously, the exact files you create depend on the nature of the documents in your project. The benefit of this approach is that all documents of one type are in the same place. The drawback is that each document might contain information about several different topics.

The second approach is to create files for separate topics. For example, you would create files for product specifications, advertising campaigns, sales force, branch offices and so on. Again, the exact nature of the files clearly depends on your project. The benefit of this approach is that all the information about each subject is in the same file. The drawback is that a document may also contain other information as well so that there is much irrelevant information in each file. And if a document contains information on more than one topic you have to photocopy it and place it in two or more files, so you multiply the amount of paper you are handling.

One way to overcome the drawbacks of both filing approaches, and to gain a firmer grip on your research material, is to cross-reference it as you gather it. Depending on your predilection, you can do this using a simple card file or a computer. Using a computer may involve learning a special piece of database or indexing software. So the software option is only worth pursuing for large projects - unless you already own and know how to use the software.

If you adopt the first approach - filing documents by document type - you give each file a title (for example, interview notes) and number each document in it sequentially starting at one. Then you create a topic card for each topic and reference them to the document file number. For example, suppose you are developing a report on marketing in Europe, you could develop topic cards for each European country in your report. Each entry on the card should give brief details (not more than 10 words) about the nature of the information to be found in the referenced document. For example, an entry might read: "France: government sales statistics quoted in FT article press cuttings file, document number 17."

In any sizeable research project you should not underestimate the value of adopting this approach. Not only will you find it easier to access your research materials when you come to write your report, but the act of cross-referencing them will give you a much better understanding of the subject.

Sifting the evidence

If the report you are preparing is a medium or large one, you will soon realise, as you continue your research, that you are building a range of different kinds of information. You could have statistics, interview notes, press cuttings, extracts from books and reports, completed questionnaires and survey forms, comments from members of the public, submissions from fellow managers or outside bodies and so on and so on. Out of this disparate material you must construct your report. Where do you begin?

The starting point is to sift information that is relevant from that which is irrelevant or unimportant. The cross-referencing exercise described above will help you do this. Next you need to decide, from the relevant material, what is important and what less so. Not all the information has the same weight.

At this point, you should clearly have in mind the purpose of your report. This purpose is the lodestar which will guide you to the material of special value. As you study the material, you will find you are faced with a mass of facts and opinions. Looking at the facts, you should ask yourself: which are the facts that really matter? Are there certain key facts that clearly stand out as more important than others? Are the sources you consulted agreed about the facts? Are there surprising facts which were not expected and which might change your views?

Studying the opinions is also important. Not all opinions carry the same weight. You need to evaluate the opinions expressed by the sources you consulted in a critical way. Do some opinions carry more weight than others because they derive from greater knowledge or experience of the subject? Are some opinions coloured by self-interest? Do people's opinions on particular topics generally agree or disagree? Are there any unexpected opinions which ought to be considered more carefully? Do the opinions change your view about the purpose of the report? These questions give just a flavour of the way in which you should approach the opinions you have been given.

As you consider and evaluate the facts and opinions you have gathered, you also need to think what you are going to do with the information. What you do will be largely determined by the purpose of your report. In chapter 1, we defined seven main purposes for a report. If the purpose of your report is to provide information, you will summarise the facts and opinions in a logical sequence. If the purpose is to provide a record, you will summarise the main points together with any action taken on them, as a source of reference to be used in the future. If the purpose is to answer a specific query, you will provide as much information as is needed to answer that query fully so that the reader should not need to ask for any further information.

If the purpose of your report is to recommend a decision or decisions, your task is rather more complex. You need to formulate your recommendations first. Then you will marshall the facts and opinions you need to justify the recommendations you have made. Similarly, if the purpose of your report is to influence opinion, you must decide on the conclusions you reach before you draft your report. Then you marshall the facts and opinions to lead up logically to those conclusions. If the purpose of your report is to gain publicity, you must decide which aspects you most wish to see publicised. Then you must make those the centre-piece of your report and build the other facts and opinions around them. If the purpose of your report is to meet a statutory obligation, you must make sure that you have included information to meet all the requirements laid down by the body to which you will submit it.

In every case, have the purpose of the report always at the front of your mind. And throughout the process of sifting your research, ask yourself: which is the material that best helps me achieve the report's purpose? (There is advice about writing the report in the next chapter.)

Sound arguments

If you are drafting the kind of report that is putting a point of view or making recommendations, you want people to agree with your conclusions. In achieving this, you need to bear three points in mind.

First, make sure that recommendations and conclusions are fully supported by the evidence in your report. Does the evidence you have provided really support the recommendation? Are there any logical flaws in your arguments? Is the evidence you have provided to support your recommendations complete and up to date? Does your recommendation go further than the evidence warrants? If you quoted expert opinions to support your recommendations, are there expert opinions that could be quoted against them? If you used examples to support your argument are they typical?

Secondly, make sure that all the evidence you provide to support your conclusions or recommendations is completely accurate. Opponents of your views will search for flaws in your report in order to undermine it. They will seize on inaccuracies or half-truths with glee. Have you checked all the facts you quote with the primary source? (If you gleaned the fact from a secondary source, it might be wrong.) As your argument progresses, is each point supported by accurate facts? Have you, by accident or design, left out any facts that clearly undermine your recommendations or conclusions? (Perhaps you should include them and explain why you still arrived at your conclusion.)

Thirdly, have in mind the outer-most boundaries of acceptable recommendations or conclusions to the readers of the report. In other words, keep your feet on the ground. You may think that the evidence in your report indicates that the company's product has no future and that, therefore, the company should go into liquidation, but this is unlikely to commend itself to the board of directors if it expected a report on future product strategy. You need to ask yourself a number of questions. What range of recommendations would be acceptable to the recipients of this report? Do their views rule out of bounds any particular recommendations? Will they be more predisposed to certain recommendations than others? All this does not mean that you should only present recommendations that your bosses will find immediately pleasing and acceptable, but that you should have a healthy awareness of the opinions and political forces at work in your organisation.

Working with a team

You may find yourself producing a report as part of a working party or team. Although this might be the only way of producing a large report, it raises other issues which you need to consider. For example, you need to agree with other members of your working party how the report will be compiled and the recommendations decided.

It helps if the working party has a clear idea about the purpose of the report right from the outset. The working party needs to understand what its recommendations must seek to achieve. For example, if the working party is set up by the district council to consider the provision of leisure facilities in Anytown, it needs to understand the constraints on any possible recommendations, such as the money that can be spent and the staff available to implement the recommendations. There is no point suggesting the building of an Olympic sports centre if the budget will only run to a kiddies" playground in the park. If all members of the working party understand the constraints on their recommendations, whole swathes of possible disagreements are removed right from the start.

The next point is to make sure that all members of the working party keep in touch with the general direction of the research as the project proceeds. This is especially important if members of the team are working on different parts of the research. You should make sure that the working party meets regularly to review the progress of each member's research area. Each member of the working party should be invited to explain the progress he has made and the significance he attaches to his findings. Then you should invite the working party to discuss those findings briefly. In this way, the working party starts to acquire a kind of collective understanding of the information as its work progresses. If this process runs smoothly, you should find that as the project nears its completion, most working party members are coming at the recommendations "from the same direction".

Inevitably, however, disagreements will arise. How should these be reconciled? The starting point is to understand the basis of each person's point of view. If you can show that the factual basis of one person's point of view is at fault, then the reason for the disagreement may disappear. But not all disagreements are like that. Fundamentally, disagreements arise because people view matters from a unique perception based on their own experience and understanding of what is significant and valuable. You cannot hope to change this kind of life-view that each person has. Nor should you. It is the reason why each person's opinion is valuable even if you disagree with it.

At the end of the day, disagreements in a working party about recommendations for a report can be settled in one of four ways:

1. *By a majority vote*. Strength: seen to be democratic. Weakness: not every choice has equal weight. Some know more about the topic than others.

2. *By accepting the decision of the chairman*. Strength: provides an outcome that the chairman can defend when the report goes public. Weakness: may leave a substantial body of dissatisfied working party members.

3. *By accepting the decision of the individual responsible for compiling that part of the report*. Strength: provides an expert view. Weakness: not all expert views are wise or sensible.

4. *By a compromise*. Strength: a compromise may satisfy everybody. Weakness: a compromise may dissatisfy everybody.

To summarise:

• Organise an effective filing and cross-reference system for research materials.
• Take account of the factors that bear on the recommendations

you can realistically make.

• Establish procedures to encourage team members to work together effectively.

.

CHAPTER 5

WRITING TO INFORM AND CONVINCE

A REPORT DISSECTED

When you pick up a report, you expect a document which is structured in a particular way and written in a clear style. As we have seen, a report should have a clear purpose. Giving a report its structure helps you to achieve that purpose by making the information in the report more accessible to the readers. There is no one structure that is suitable for all reports because reports differ greatly in length and complexity. However, you can structure any report around several common elements. These are:

Title page. The title page is like that in a book. It contains the title of the report, its author, the date the report was published and the body that published it. What kind of title should you give your report? That depends on its purpose. If the purpose is to provide information, a record, answer a specific query or recommend a decision, you should choose a descriptive and functional title. For example, *New Office Block: recommendations for decoration and fitting out.* Note how this title contains the main gist of the report in the first three words followed by a phrase amplifying the exact purpose of the report after the colon. This is an effective style for many report titles.

If the purpose of the report is to influence opinion or gain publicity, you might want to choose a more imaginative title designed to catch attention from people who don't have to read it. For example, the Prince of Wales' Business Leaders' Forum adopted this two tier approach for a report about company ethics:

Corporate Reputation in Tomorrow's Marketplace: A survey of the opinions and expectations of the young business leaders of today and tomorrow.

The two-tier approach works well because it enables you to compose an attention-grabbing main title in not more than half a dozen words and then amplify it with a longer explanatory phrase underneath. In this case both are designed to attract the attention of those the report wants to influence.

You can use the same approach for reports designed to gain publicity. For example:

The European Lunchtime Report
A comparison of working lunchtime habits in Europe.

Published by a leading catering company, it surveyed the different lunchtime habits and favoured dishes across the continent in a way designed to make a good story for journalists.

Contents. The contents page comes after the title page and provides a chronological list of the chapters or sections in the report and the page number on which each begins. In the shortest of reports, you might want to omit a contents page. In longer reports, you need to decide how much detail to put on the contents page. For example, do you want to list only the main sections of the report or subsections as well? As a general rule, listing sections only is sufficient for a medium-sized report. Include sub-sections in a longer report.

Terms of reference. The next section to include is the terms of reference of the report. This should be formally stated, often as it was given to you, as a means of showing readers the basis on which you approached the task. If the report was compiled by a working party or committee, you will also list the members and their job functions/titles after the terms of reference. In some cases, you may wish to include this information as part of the introduction (see below) rather than as a separate section.

Summary. All but the very shortest of reports need a summary at the start. The summary has two purposes. The first is as a reference for the reader who has the time to read nothing but the summary. The second is to over-view the report for the reader who plans to study it in detail. The summary gives him a high-level view of the whole report before he starts to consider each section in turn. The length of the summary will be relative to the length of the report. For a short report, the summary might occupy no more than three or four paragraphs. For a long report, the summary might take up three or four pages.

Plainly, you should not write the summary until you have written the rest of the report. Even so, summary writing is difficult. What should you put in and what should you leave out? In general, the summary should describe the main topic areas that the report deals with, often from the point of view of the conclusion you reached about that topic. For example, suppose you have compiled a report about the feasibility of moving your company to a new office block. Your report will have a section dealing with how each department will move in a phased programme from its existing accommodation to the new quarters. Such a section could run for a score or more pages, but the summary should be something like:

• The company should adopt a phased programme so that each

department moves in successive weeks in the order accounts, marketing, central services and despatch.

This probably summarises everything you need to say about this section of the report, although the detail of how the departments will move and why they should move in that order will be contained in the main body of the report.

Introduction. The purpose of the introduction is to describe how you set about your task. You tell the report's reader how you interpreted your terms of reference and how you set about researching the subject matter for your report. You reveal briefly what is to follow, and perhaps you explain why you have placed the information in the order you have chosen. You do not need to embark on the meat of your evidence or your findings in the introduction. Indeed, you do best to keep your introduction as brief as possible. This section is often the best place to put information about the report's terms of reference and working party membership. You may also wish to use the introduction to acknowledge and thank any people who have helped you especially in providing information for the report.

Evidence and findings. You now move into the main body of your report, where you start to present evidence and findings. How you do this depends on the nature of the information in your report. But you should consider a few general principles. First, does your information fall into a naturally logical order? Often, this will be the case. If so, make sure you present the information in that order. Secondly, if there is not an obviously logical order to the information, think about your material from the reader's point of view. What will it be most helpful for him to know about first? Is understanding one point dependent on knowing another?

If so, make sure the information appears in that order. Finally, if you still cannot decide on the most appropriate order to present your information, try out several alternatives. Make two or three outlines each with the information in a different order. Does one of the outlines stand out as more effective than the others? Which of the outlines is most helpful to the reader?

In the case of a large report, you may want to divide up the evidence and findings into chapters or sections. This is especially helpful if the information falls naturally into several main sections. Dividing a large report into chapters helps both the writer and the reader. The chapters provide a logical framework for organising the information and writing the report. They also provide the reader with some natural break points in his study of the report.

In any event, you should take care to present your information accurately and unambiguously. You should make sure that you explain the provenance of important pieces of information. For example, if you quote facts about the future growth rates in your industry, mention the source of the figures, perhaps a business school or industry association. By presenting the sources of your information in this kind of transparent way, you enhance the authority of your report.

Footnotes are a useful tool for referencing information. They enable you to provide detailed facts about the source of a piece of information without interrupting the flow of your argument. But use footnotes sparingly - not more than two or three to a page – or they become irritating to the reader.

Analysis. When you have presented your evidence and findings, you move on to present an analysis of the information. Depending on the nature of the report, you may do this as you present the findings so that the evidence and the analysis are interwoven.

Alternatively, you may prefer to present the evidence first and the analysis afterwards. It is often helpful to present the analysis separately when there is a large body of evidence. Another reason for presenting the analysis separately is when there is likely to be disagreement over the analysis - where the evidence can be interpreted in different ways. Keeping the analysis in one section (hopefully) confines the controversy to that section of the report.

On the other hand, you may want to mix the analysis with the evidence if you want to guide your readers strongly to a particular point of view. If you take this route, you need to be certain it will be acceptable to your readers. It is certainly an effective approach when you are writing a report whose main purpose is to influence opinion or gain publicity, but may be less acceptable if the purpose of the report is to provide information or recommend a decision, where the readers may want the evidence and the analysis clearly separated.

Conclusions and recommendations. Whereas analysis shows how you have interpreted the evidence, the conclusions show what you have decided or what you recommend on the basis of your analysis. The conclusions stand apart from the analysis so that your readers can see clearly what they are and decide whether to accept them. In most cases, you will present a single set of conclusions. In rarer cases, you may want to present alternative conclusions, especially if the subject matter of the report is controversial or if the evidence you have assembled is inconclusive. In these cases, perhaps the buck does not stop on your desk, and the final decisions should be taken by more senior people.

Depending on size and subject matter, this section of your report may fall into two parts. In the first part, you discuss your general conclusions. In the second part, you set out the recommendations. This is a workmanlike approach, because it avoids each recommendation becoming entangled in a large amount of justification. For example, do not write:

> In view of the over-crowding in the present office, and because of the need to expand the department, it is recommended that the accounts department moves to the new office building on 1 February 2008 and not 1 December 2007 as there is a possibility that the cabling for the new computers will not be completed.

Apart from the fact that the subordinate phrases obscure the recommendation, this approach also invites the reader to disagree with the central recommendation if he does not wholeheartedly agree with every supporting statement in the sentence. ("I think we will have the computer cabling completed by the first of December so let's move earlier.")

Ideally, each recommendation should be a single clear statement. For example, it is more effective to write:

> It is recommended that the accounts department moves to the new office building on 1 February 2008.

This presents the recommendation clearly, shorn of all its justification subtext. In any event, you have argued the reasons for your recommendation elsewhere in the report.

Appendices. There is a huge range of appendices you could include in a report, but the first point to consider is whether you should include any. Appendices can add substantially to the bulk of your report, but do they add much to the understanding of the subject matter? In other words, are the appendices adding weight without insight? As a general rule, only include an appendix if it adds useful extra information that the reader needs in order to appreciate the conclusions and recommendations you have reached.

Normally, an appendix will consist of a self-contained piece of information whose inclusion in the main body of the report would have unnecessarily diverted the reader at that point or held up the flow of the narrative or argument. An example of information that could be included in an appendix is an important piece of evidence which you considered in reaching your recommendations but which you did not want to place in the main body of the report. It could be a letter, a document or extract from a document, a table of figures, the results of a survey or many other things.

You should number every appendix and list each on the contents page. You should also cross-reference each from the main body of your text, when you deal with an issue where it might be helpful for the reader to glance at the relevant appendix.

Bibliography and sources of evidence, You will not normally include these in reports of modest size and scope. However, in a large report, perhaps one compiled by a working party, it might well be relevant to include a list of people and organisations that gave evidence to the working party. You should divide the list into those who gave evidence in person and those who sent written evidence. If you have consulted a large number of books or other reports in compiling your report, it might be helpful to provide a bibliography for the reader. For each entry in the bibliography, you give the name of the book, the author(s), the publisher and the date of publication of the edition you consulted.

Index. Again, the inclusion of an index is rare in a report, but it is something you might want to consider for a very large report – say one that runs to more than 100 pages. The index should refer not only to the people and organisations you mention in the report, but also the concepts you deal with. Study the indexes in quality non-fiction books in order to gain an idea of the different indexing styles available. Choose a style which indexes the report at the most appropriate level of detail.

Report writing step by step

Drafting a report requires the same high level of writing skills needed for any important business document. What about the specific skills of writing a report? How should you set about the task? You cannot begin to write your report until you clearly understand the conclusions and recommendations you wish to reach. Report writing is like setting off on a journey. You need to know where you are going before you depart. If you don't know where you are going, you will wander around and end up anywhere, Similarly, if you do not understand the conclusions and recommendations you want your report to reach, you will not be able to marshall the material you researched in order to support them. You will be writing without purpose or direction.

The golden rule of report writing, therefore, is: do not start writing until you know what your conclusions and recommendations will be and the reasons you have reached them. As we saw in chapter 4, this means thoroughly thinking through your material either by yourself or discussing it with other members of your working party. When you have decided on your conclusions and recommendations you are in a position to start writing the report.

You should start writing the different sections of your report in this order:

- Introduction
- Findings and evidence

- Analysis
- Conclusions and recommendations

When you have written these sections, you should review them before you go on to write any more sections. Go back over your draft text and examine it with a critical eye. Ask yourself some hard questions. Does the introduction accurately describe what is to come - or does it make promises which are not fulfilled in the rest of the report? Have I included all the evidence that is relevant? Have I presented the evidence fairly? Have I given the correct weight to the most important evidence? Have I presented the evidence in the most effective order?

Next question your analysis. Is my analysis justified by the evidence? Have I gone farther than the evidence justifies? Have I overlooked important parts of the evidence? Do the different parts of my analysis hang coherently together or do I contradict myself?

Finally, study your conclusions and recommendations. Are my conclusions justified by my analysis? Is the link from evidence through analysis to conclusions clear in the case of every conclusion? Are my recommendations sensible and reasonable? Are any of the recommendations ambiguous? Have I expressed my recommendations clearly? Are these recommendations likely to be acceptable to the person or group which commissioned the report? If not, should I add extra evidence to support them and clearer analysis to punch home why I believe they are the correct recommendations?

When you have been through this exercise, you will probably want to redraft some of what you have written. You may even want to redraft all of it. Do this before writing any other parts of the report. When you have a second draft of the introduction, evidence, analysis, conclusions and recommendations, subject it again to the critical questioning described above. If you believe it passes, then it is time to draft the other parts of the report:

- Title
- Contents
- Summary

You should also add appendices, the source of evidence and bibliography (if applicable) and the index (if applicable). When you have done that, you need to look at the whole report again for a final check. Does the whole report serve the purpose for which it is intended? You should certainly trust your own judgement to answer this question, but it is also valuable to seek the opinions of trusted colleagues. Ask people whose judgement you respect and who will look at the report in the light of its purpose. Seek the views of people who are able to take the broader view rather than those whose only contribution will be to point out an errant comma on page 73.

Other people's views will certainly be valuable in helping you to make a judgement about the shape and wording of your final report. Indeed, you may want to make further changes based on their suggestions. But be in no doubt: if it is your report it must, ultimately, be your judgement which decides how the report is presented. So do not be talked into making changes you do not believe in. If challenged, you will find it hard to justify them at a later date.

Writing as a team
What happens if you are producing your report as the head of a working party? Does the whole team write the report? Definitely

not. You should avoid the situation in which people sit round trying to draft the report sentence by sentence. The working party should appoint a rapporteur whose task will be to produce the different drafts of the report under the direction of the working party.

The working party should discuss each section of the report in sufficient detail for the rapporteur to have a clear idea of the consensus of the team. When the rapporteur has produced the first draft, the working party should discuss it in fairly general terms (no nit-picking detail at this stage) with a view to producing a second draft which more closely meets the working party's aims.

It is at second draft stage that the working party should go through the report paragraph by paragraph, making any fine adjustments that are needed. Then the rapporteur produces a third draft. At this stage, the report should be close to the finished version. It needs to be critically examined (perhaps by the working party chairman and the rapporteur) against the points mentioned above. As a result, the rapporteur may make some final changes. When the fourth and final draft of the report comes back to the working party, it should be in a form which the members can approve without further detailed discussion.

To summarise:

- Understand the different sections that could appear in a report and choose those most appropriate.
- Approach the drafting of a report in a logical way.
- Evaluate the first draft with a critical eye and redraft where necessary.
- Appoint a rapporteur to draft a report for a working party.

CHAPTER 6

DESIGN, LAYOUT AND PRODUCTION

WORDS ON A PAGE

When all is said and done, your report ends up as words on a page. (True, there may be a few charts and diagrams, and we will come to those in a moment.) No matter how well researched the evidence, how wise the analysis and how compelling the conclusions, you will undermine it all if you do not present the information accessibly. This means the report must be easy to handle and straightforward to read. In other words, it must be fit for the purpose.

You need to think about this even before you start to write the text because some of the issues will affect how you approach the writing. It is possible that your organisation has a house style for reports which deals with such issues as page layout, paragraph numbering and so on. If so, you need to obtain a copy of this house style and study it before you start writing. If not, you need to decide how to lay out the report before you start writing in order to ensure consistency of approach throughout the document.

One of the issues you need to consider is whether or not you will number the paragraphs and, if so, which numbering convention you will adopt. The point of paragraph numbering is to make it easier to refer to parts of the report during discussions. In a report of two or three pages, you might choose to dispense with paragraph numbering. In a longer report, it is essential to number paragraphs. There are three main numbering conventions to choose from:

Sequential numbering. With this approach, you number the first paragraph 1, the second 2 and so on through the report. It has the advantage of being simple and straightforward. But it has some drawbacks. For example, it is not possible to show how a number of paragraphs are logically grouped together. Nor is it useful if you want to include sub-paragraphs within paragraphs.

Mixed numbers and letters. With this approach, you number main paragraphs with Arabic numerals and sub-paragraphs with lower case letters. You use Roman numerals to pick out further divisions with sub-paragraphs. So numbering would proceed like this: 1 a i, 1 a ii, 1 b i, 2 a i, 2 b i, 2 b ii, etc. The advantage of this system is that it helps you to group information logically together and to make the different points stand out. In addition, by making a small indent for the lettered sub-paragraphs and a larger indent for Roman numeral sub-paragraphs, you guide the eye down the page and provide visual variety, breaking up large slabs of text. However, this approach is not always suitable for a long report and it can become cumbersome if there is a large number of sub-paragraphs within paragraphs.

Decimal numbering. With this approach, main paragraphs receive a number, first-level paragraphs a number after a first decimal point, and second-level paragraphs a number after a second decimal point. So numbering proceeds like this: 1.1.1, 1.1.2, 1.2.1, 1.3.1,2.1.1,2.1.2, etc. As with the mixed numbering and lettering approach, the same points about indenting apply. The advantage of this approach is that it is severely logical. But again, it is not necessarily suitable for really long reports for the same reasons as the mixed numbers and letters approach. In addition, it can prove confusing to implement in practice – should that paragraph be 12.2.3 or 12.3. 2?

Charts, diagrams and pictures

Many reports could be greatly improved with the intelligent use of charts, diagrams and pictures. Yet too often writers overlook this potentially important ingredient of a report. Pictorial devices are most effective when they work with the text in order to help make a point more powerfully. They are least effective when the writer includes them for no other reason than that he thinks it makes the report look "nicer".

There are two kinds of charts that are especially useful in reports – those that illustrate relationships and those that illustrate ratios. Charts that illustrate relationships include:

Figure 1 An Organisation Chart

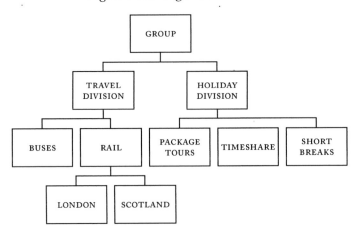

Organisation chart. This is a chart that shows the relationship of one part of the organisation to another. It generally consists of boxes linked by lines often (but not always) arranged in a nested hierarchy. The organisation chart is effectively a high-level map of an organisation.

Block diagram, This is a generally simple chart which is often

Figure 2 A block diagram

used to show the order in which activities must be carried out to complete a process. It consists of a start block, and number of blocks each of which represents a self-contained activity, and a stop block. The block diagram is an effective way of illustrating the workings of a process.

Flow chart, There are several different types of flow chart. They are drawn using a library of standard shapes, where each shape represents a different type of activity – for example a decision or an action. A standard flowchart (page 174) is used to show the relationship between the different activities in a business process. A functional flowchart also pictures the activities in a process but, in addition, shows how those activities move between different work units. A geographical flowchart shows how activities move between different geographical locations. All of these are valuable aids to help describe the workings of complex business processes.

Charts that illustrate ratios are normally used to display numerical results and are common to reports. The main types are:

Graph. Figures plotted against two axes – a horizontal time axis and vertical value axis. Straight lines link the intersection points. More than one line can be placed on the same graph. Different coloured lines can be used to show the relationships between different sets of figures – for example, this year's sales compared with last year's.

Histogram, Otherwise known as a bar chart. The horizontal axis is used to plot the information type, for example, sales regions such as south, north, east and west. The vertical axis plots the amount. Bars of appropriate height are used to display the measure. Again, bars can be grouped together – for example in twos, to show last year's budget and actual for each region. Different colours or shading helps to make the histogram easier to follow.

Figure 3 A simple process flowchart

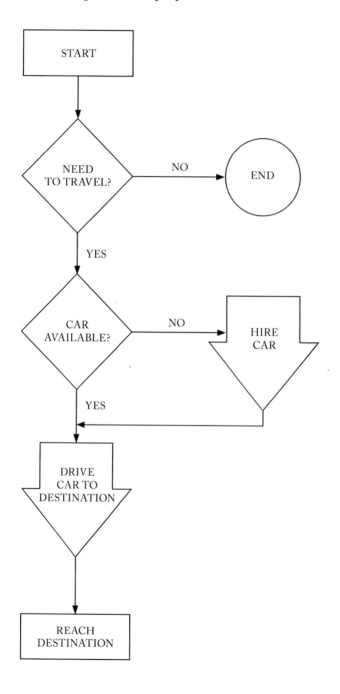

Pie chart. This is used to show the proportions of a whole taken by each part. A circle is divided into slices, each slice in its correct ratio to the whole. A pie chart is often used in an annual report to show the proportion of turnover or profit earned by each division or subsidiary of the company.

Pictogram. This displays numerical information with appropriate pictures which are used in proportion to the size of the numbers they represent. The pictures are usually displayed along a horizontal scale. For example, a pictogram showing the value of agricultural production in the UK might use pictures of pigs, cows, sheep, and so on to represent the different kinds of livestock. The number of pictures of each would be in proportion to the value of production.

Beyond these two categories of charts, there is a wide range of diagrams and other pictorial matter that might form part of your report. These could include maps, plans, drawings of equipment or apparatus, photographs, and so on. In deciding what pictorial matter to include, be guided by three principles. First, does it advance the purpose of the report? Secondly, does it add value to the text? Thirdly, does it enhance the appearance of the report?

Getting into print

Finally, you must consider how the report is to be produced in multiple copies. You will need to give some preliminary thought to this at the outset because it could influence the way you produce the text. At the simplest level, you will produce just two copies of your report – one for yourself and one for the person who requested it. At higher levels, the report's circulation could run into hundreds, even thousands of copies.

Whether you choose to write the text in longhand and then have it keyboarded, or whether you keyboard it yourself, we start from the assumption that the text of your report exists on a computer. (If the text doesn't exist on a computer, you should certainly arrange to install one. Producing a report without a computer is now rather like tilling a field with a horse-drawn plough.)

In fact, information technology has now advanced to the point where it is possible to produce reports with typeset text, complex tables and graphics – as well as colour photographs – on your own PC or laptop. Just how sophisticated you want to make your report depends on the nature of the project – and your skill at using the software. But with so many facilities now available, there is a danger of becoming so entranced with them that you lose sight of what ought to be your main focus – the content of your report. In cases where you are planning to have your report printed, you should be able to e-mail the file you produce to the printer who will use it to print the report. One word of warning, files do occasionally become corrupted so that they produce small errors. You should ask the printer for a proof before the report finally goes to press. If you work in a company with sophisticated document copying equipment, you may even be able to send your file direct to the copying machine and have it printed. The point is that IT now provides a whole new range of possibilities so that you can present even a small report with a style and polish that would have been impossible in the days of the old steam typewriter.

Next, you need to decide the most effective way of producing the required number of copies of your report. There are three issues that will bear on your decision: the size of the report, the number of copies you plan to produce (the "print run"), and whether the report contains any pictorial matter. There are three main options for producing your report:

Running the copies directly off a computer printer. This is the best approach when you have a smallish report and require only a handful of copies. However, once you get above a total of, say, about 100 pages to print, this approach becomes rather cumbersome even with a laser printer.

Running a master copy off the computer's printer and then photocopying (including specialist high-speed photocopying). This is an option for large reports with quite large print runs, especially if high-speed copying services are used. For example, several hundred copies of a report of up to 200 or 300 pages could realistically be produced by a high-speed copying service at prices which are competitive with printing. There are now services which can take the text straight from e-mailed files or CD-Roms and produce the finished reports. However, the main drawback of high-speed copying is that it does not give as high a quality as printing. This is especially true if the report contains complex diagrams or charts with large solid blocks.

Producing a master copy on the computer and printing, This is the option to choose when the report has to be produced to a high print quality (including possible photographs and diagrams) in large numbers. For smallish print runs, it is often the most expensive option but it produces the best results. However, for large print runs of any-sized report, printing is often the most economic option. If the standard of presentation is important – for example, in a report prepared to influence opinion – then printing is the choice to make.

Along with the method of printing, you also need to make a decision about the binding of the report. Again, your decision will be determined by the nature of the report. The options are:

Stapling. The simplest approach for small reports with small circulations. A cheap and cheerful approach – and looks it – but perfectly acceptable for a wide range of internal reports. Becomes ineffective when reports get large and the staples don't go through all the sheets. Then consider:

Treasury tags. Can hold together up to about 200 pages, depending on the length of the tag. But reports bound this way are not always easy to handle, especially if they are large – the pages slip about and tear loose from the tag.

Ready-made folders. These come in a variety of formats available from your friendly neighbourhood stationer. They are often comparatively pricey, typically £2 or more a time – and sometimes not all that effective (especially the ones where you slide the pages of your report between a groove-shaped piece of plastic. Open the pages too wide and the whole thing falls apart.) However, if you have a small report and small print run, a ready made folder could provide the answer.

Comb-binding. The left hand margin of each page is punched with a line of rectangular holes. Then a circular comb is inserted through them to hold the lot together – often with cardboard or acetate covers. You can buy machines to do this from as little as £80. Alternatively, you can get your reports bound at any instant print shop which provides the service and most do. Comb binding is an excellent option for any report of about 30-300 pages as it makes the report comparatively easy to handle and is durable.

Binding. This is the option to choose if your report has been printed. The report can be saddle-stitched – stapled or sewn down the central gutter between the centre left and right hand pages. Saddle stitching is suitable for reports of up to about 80 pages. Alternatively, you can choose perfect binding – where the pages are glued or stitched in groups at the spine so that the bound report assumes a block shape, like this book. Perfect binding is more expensive than saddle stitching but provides a higher quality result. However, perfect binding is generally impractical below about 32 pages.

To summarise:

- Consider the best way to layout your text on the page for easy reading.
- Use diagrams and charts when they add value to the text.
- Select the most appropriate printing and binding methods for each report.

Chapter 7

Any other business

Post-report moves

So you have completed and delivered your report. Is that it? Not entirely. Your report could be the ingredient needed to set off many different kinds of reactions. You need to be prepared. For this reason you should not sweep all your source material into the wastepaper basket the day after you deliver the report. You might need it again.

What could happen? You might be asked to provide further information on the report in general or a specific section of it. Alternatively, you might be asked to provide a follow-up report. You could be challenged to justify some of the conclusions or recommendations you have made in the report. You may even be asked to present the report's main findings to a meeting. These and other possibilities mean that you should continue to regard the report as a live project in your work schedule for a reasonable period after you have delivered it.

However, perhaps none of these things happen. Perhaps you hear nothing. Does that mean you can quietly forget the project? Preferably not. You should seek some feedback on the report from those who received it. Did it deal with the issues they wanted addressed? Did the report meet their expectations? Were there any issues not dealt with which they would have liked to be covered? Have they taken any decisions based on the report?

Answers to questions such as these are important because they help you to evaluate how successfully you completed the report project. No matter how many reports you write, there are always new lessons to learn.

You can learn from failures as well as successes. Why did they not act on the report? Did I present enough evidence? Was the argument logical and convincing? Were my recommendations realistic? Did they have a "hidden agenda" which I failed to appreciate and account for in the report? Did the report fall victim to internal politics which I failed to appreciate and allow for? Was the report simply not as readable as it should have been? The report writer who continually improves asks questions such as these about any major report project.

It is easy to understand why a business manager regards the call for a report as just another chore. In fact, if you regard report writing as an unwelcome chore, you will probably not be very good at it. Your boredom and sense of tedium will tend to show through in the report. But the manager who gains a reputation for producing effective reports will help himself as well as his organisation. Most managers, if pushed, can produce some sort of report, which perhaps just about fits the bill. But the manager that produces a report which stands out as well above average, stands out as above average himself. He marks himself in the eyes of his bosses as someone with a valuable and useful skill. The quality of his thinking also shows through in the report – and that can commend itself to his bosses as well. In short, the writer of quality reports is doing no harm to his career prospects.

Six steps to success
What benchmarks can you use to judge the success of a report? If your report can measure up to the following six qualities, it should

be as close to perfect as you can make it.

1. *Actionable.* There are many purposes for a report but, in most cases, the recipient of the report will want to take some kind of action based on its contents. So the successful report presents information in a way that guides the reader to action. There are several ways it can do this – for example, by providing clear and sensible recommendations. In an actionable report, the information is organised so that the reader can immediately see those issues that require action and those which provide background. The tone and style of an actionable report is upbeat. It reinforces the reader's confidence to take the decisions that are needed.

2. *Tailored.* A report can, conceivably, have a readership of one or one million. Whichever the number, in the tailored report information is organised to make it accessible and relevant to the readership. This involves the writer tailoring both the information and the style in which it is written to the readers. In the case of some reports – for example, regular reports containing performance information – it may involve tailoring the report to an exact specification laid down by the reader. In all cases, a well tailored report will make the reader say: "This is just what I need. "

3. *Focus.* The focus comes from a clear understanding of the purpose of the report. Focus means addressing that purpose in every page and every paragraph. In a well-focused report, all the information is assembled to support the main purpose of the report. The narrative or argument of the report drives forward steadily from page to page. There are no time-wasting digressions. Background information is kept to the minimum needed to provide the reader with enough understanding of the subject. The purpose of the report shines through from the first sentence to the last.

4. *Timely.* A successful report is delivered on time. This may

seem obvious, but plenty of reports arrive on the reader's desk too late to be useful. If the report is to be used as the basis of a decision, the reader needs a reasonable time to study it before he takes the decision. How long depends both on the length of the report and the complexity and importance of the decisions. Many people may have to discuss the report before they take the decision. That is a potentially lengthy process. It is the job of the report writer to present the report in plenty of time so that the decision-making process is not rushed.

5. *Organised.* In a successful report the contents are carefully and helpfully organised. The information is divided into logical sections, an appropriate paragraph numbering system helps the reader to reference the information and illuminating charts and diagrams are provided wherever they add value to the text. Often, an organised report is the output of an organised report project. If the writer approaches his task logically, conducts his research systematically and thoroughly, writes his report carefully, the sense of organisation will show through in the finished report. Muddle begets muddle – and it shows.

6. *Reliable.* Finally, a successful report inspires confidence. It possesses the five qualities mentioned above. The reader can sense the authority of the report radiating off its pages. It gives him confidence to take decisions – perhaps important decisions based on its contents.

Reports in the computer age

So far in this book, we have discussed reports as paper documents. Increasingly, they will be electronic "documents" in a computer. As we have already mentioned, most reports are now written on computers. If a report is written on a computer, it is only a short step to reading it on a computer. Admittedly, it will be a long time before managers want to read a long document on a computer screen because that can prove rather tiring to the eyes. And a paper document is more portable – it can be read on the plane or train – although the growing acceptance of laptop computers is even undermining that argument.

However, the computer presents all kinds of report producing possibilities that paper never had. For example, reports can be assembled more quickly from information already held in electronic files. Using report generation software, it is possible to pull different kinds of information out of different databases and then combine it in a new format in a single report. Computer graphics help the report writer to produce full colour graphics more cheaply and more easily than was ever the case before.

It is even possible to produce a computer-based "multimedia" report. This uses special software to allow the report compiler to include text, graphics, photographs, motion video and voice in a report which the viewer can access from his own computer. For the manager clever enough to spot the opportunity and master the technology, multimedia offers the prospect of producing exciting new types of reports which can present information in a far more compelling way than ever before.

Like most other aspects of the business world, the report, too, will undergo dramatic transformation. But despite changes in technology, most of the principles of report production remain the same. Even a report produced with the latest glitzy technology and the most exciting visual effects will fail if it does not serve the purpose for which it is intended.

In the end, it is human judgement which will be the most important ingredient in reports. And that will be as precious a commodity as ever.

To summarise:

- Keep your background information for a reasonable period after delivering a report.
- Understand the six factors that make a successful report.
- Investigate the potential of computers to deliver new kinds of reports.
-

Appendix

Useful books

General writing guides:

New Oxford Spelling Dictionary: The Writers' and Editors' Guide to Spelling and Word Division (Oxford University Press). Good dictionary choice for workplace writers.

Fowler's Modern English Usage by Henry Fowler, Simon Winchester (Oxford Language Classics). The classic wise witty guide to using English elegantly.

Mind the Gaffe: The Penguin Guide to Common Errors in English, by R L Trask. Does what it says on the cover.

Eats, Shoots and Leaves: the Zero Tolerance Approach to Punctuation, by Lynn Truss (Profile Books). Amusing comments about commas and semi-colons.

Usage and Abusage, originally by Eric Partridge. Latest version edited by Janet Whitcut (Penguin Reference). A scholarly reference work on the correct use of the English language.

The Complete Plain Words, originally by Sir Ernest Gowers. Latest version revised by Sidney Greenbaum and Janet Whitcut (Penguin). Takes its philosophy from a seventeenth century quotation: "As if plain words, useful and intelligible instructions, were not as good for an esquire, or one that is in commission from the King, as for him that holds the plough."

Acknowledgements

The examples of bad writing on pages 1, 2, 6, 8, 9 and 10 are reproduced by kind permission of the:

Plain English Campaign
PO Box 3
New Mills
High Peak
SK22 4QP

Telephone: 01663 744409
Website: www.plainenglish.co.uk
E-mail: info@plainenglish.co.uk

INDEX